Healing Words

A Journey Through the Ladder UPP™

A selection of works submitted by those healing from traumatic events via creative writing based upon exercises from Silouan Green's The Ladder UPP™ workbook.

Contributing Authors:

Dawn Cunningham, B.G.S. and M.A.

Denise K. Buhr

J. Vaughan

John D. Hannigan

ML Wissing

First Edition

Cover design by ©DJMadameNoir
www.facebook.com/DJMadameNoir
www.DJMadameNoir.weebly.com

Healing Words 2017
Contains the works of:
Denise K. Buhr
Dawn Cunningham
John D. Hannigan
J. Vaughan
ML Wissing
and other members of the Ladder Upp™ group of Indiana University-Purdue University Fort Wayne (IPFW)

© Believer Creations Publishing, LLC 2017

ISBN-10: 1976189632
ISBN-13: 978-1976189630

A Note from Believer Creations Publishing LLC

No part of this publication may be reproduced, stored in a retrieval system, or transmitted, in any form by any means, electronic, mechanical, photocopying, recording, or otherwise without the prior permission of the authors.

This work may contain submissions that are a part of other works by the authors. These are included via permission.

This contains both writings of fiction and nonfiction.

Some of the names, characters, events, places, or incidents either are the product of the author's imagination or are used fictitiously, and any resemblance to persons, living or dead, business establishments, events, or locales, is entirely coincidental. The publisher does not have any control over and does not assume responsibility for author or third-party websites or their content.

Please do not participate in or encourage piracy of copyrighted materials in violation of the author's rights. Purchase only authorized editions.

Thank you and good reading!

The authors and publisher hold no responsibility for any flashbacks, memories, or feelings experienced while reading this book.

If you are experiencing troubling feelings, we advise you to talk to someone. Talking to others is what helped the authors. You do not have to go through it alone.

National Suicide Prevention Lifeline
1-800-273-TALK (8255)

Crisis Text Line
TEXT "CONNECT" TO 741741

Rape, Abuse, and Incest National Network (RAINN)
(800) 656-HOPE

Domestic Violence
800-799-7233 (SAFE)

Alcohol & Drug Abuse Hotline
(800) 729-6686

Contributors

This anthology contains selected works of the following members of the Indiana University-Purdue University Fort Wayne The Ladder UPP™ Creative Writing Group:

John D. Hannigan

John D. Hannigan was born in Boston, Massachusetts on April 19th 1935. He enlisted in United States Army and served until October 1964. His military assignments included Army Security Agency, National Security Agency and State Department support of worldwide Embassies and overseas travel including Japan, Korea, Eritrea and Ethiopia. He worked as a government employee from October 1964 until May 1966, working for the National Security Agency and in the Department of Defense Government Industry contracting for Defense Contractors from May 1968 until retirement in August 2005. He served in Integrated Logistics Management specializing in Classified Projects due to his Military and Government background.

Hannigan had two years of college classes in Engineering, Logistics, Quality, Reliability, and Qualitative Time Measurement for Classified Communications Systems.

Upon retirement in 2005, he worked to support veterans, their families, and their welfare. He currently facilitates three Veterans' Honor Roll for the State of Indiana and Community Action Programs. He is a member of the American Legion, Disabled Veterans of America, Korean War Veterans Association, Old Crows Association, Society of Logistics Engineers, and Allen County Genealogy Society of Indiana.

Hannigan journaled most of his adult life on the topic of his experiences in military, government, and industry. He then enrolled in Ladder UPP™ writing for Post-Traumatic Stress classes at Indiana University- Purdue University Fort Wayne,

Indiana. He says the group helped him to express his inner frustrations from military service, government employment, and personal tragedies he incurred during his life, and that he became a better writer when he expressed his inner feelings in a writing format to be published later.

Hannigan is married with eight children, nine grandchildren, and nine great grand-children.

ML Wissing

Michele Wissing is a college student currently enrolled in Indiana University-Purdue University Fort Wayne. She is majoring in both Legal Studies and General Studies, as well as minoring in Psychology.

She is an Iraq War Veteran, who served her country for over seven years total in the active duty Army, Army National Guard, and Army Reserves before having to leave after her End of Term of Service date due to injuries and mental issues stemming from PTSD.

She is deeply involved in aiding others with PTSD, depression, and suicide prevention due to personal experiences and strives to assist others through writing; either through her essays, or her book *Fragments*. She is also a certified Applied Suicide Intervention Skills Training (ASIST) caregiver. She has published three books to date: *Fragments, The Game,* and *The Darkness Calls Book 1: To Hell and Back.*

She has been married six years to her husband, whom she met while they both were serving in Iraq. Her husband is currently serving in the military.

Dawn Cunningham, B.G.S. and M.A.

As an award-winning published writer with many pieces in various journals and an anthology, Dawn Cunningham uses the tool of writing to deal with issues in her life. She sees the world through the eyes of a writer, a writer who believes stories help the world keep going and live on.

The works found in this anthology by Ms. Cunningham varies from humor to pain. Post-Traumatic Stress Disorder (PTSD) affects a wide range of individuals for different reasons. She believes that if it were not for writing, sanity would not exist.

Denise K. Buhr

Denise Buhr served three years in the United States Army. After her discharge, she attended Indiana University where she received a B.A. in English and a Master's degree in Library Science.

She has worked as a children's librarian, in a chemical engineering library, and as a university archivist and arts librarian.

She is the author of a number of plays, including two published melodramas, *Mine, All Mine* and *A Penny Saved*; two commissioned works, *Her Women Were Called To Gather* and *Fighting Words: A Dialogue on Women in Combat*; and a prize-winning play about breast cancer, *Discom-BOOB-ulated*.

J. Vaughan

J. Vaughan has worked with folks who have experienced trauma for most of her professional career spanning five decades. As a trained counselor, she has assisted many individuals, couples, families, and community groups to address the aftereffects of trauma that encompass the widest variety of PTSD triggers.

Not all survivors of traumatic events react in stereotypical manners or triggers; with PTSD, it is often the "sleeping giant" that awakens just when the survivor has gained success in relationships and/or career. Like a hard-right hook from out of nowhere, PTSD can rear up to challenge the status quo and disrupt livelihoods, relationships, and work.

Vaughan has been writing most of her life, and saw The Ladder UPP™ as a means to provide more resources to help veterans, community members, siblings, spouses, and all those within reach of the IPFW campus, to find support, strength, and a voice to tell their story in a way that brings healing and hope.

She worked directly with Silouan Green to bring him to campus and gained permission to create the IPFW Ladder UPP™ Creative Writing Group.

Other Works

By Founder Silouan Green:

Sycamore Hill
Who Am I?
Ladder UPP™ Workbook

By Our Contributors:

Dawn Cunningham, B.G.S. and M.A.

The following are literary journals of publication:

Confluence: "Taking Off of Glasses" (2001 Christaine I. Seiler Award for Poetry), and other poems and flash fiction
Diagram
EWR Every Day Poems
The Voices Project
Misfit Magazine
Cliterature
Shuf Poetry
Dandelions Review
Eye to the Telescope: Ghost
Ground Fresh Thursday: "Nothing like Silence: Deafens a Mom" (finalist in GFT Press Anniversary Contest)
A Spilling of Words: A Collection of Flash Fiction, Poetry, and Creative Nonfiction (anthology)
South 85 Journal: Our Blog, a personal essay
The News-Sentinel (Fort Wayne), a letter to the editor
A performance of "Visiting the Vacant" done by Fort Wayne Dance Collective.

Denise K. Buhr

Mine, All Mine, or… From Ghost Town to Kaboom Town
A Penny Saved, or… The Widow Roostock, Fully Loded
Fighting Words: A Dialogue on "Women in Combat"

ML Wissing

Fragments
The Game
The Darkness Calls: Book 1 - To Hell and Back

Acknowledgements

Thank you to Indiana University-Purdue University Fort Wayne (IPFW) and the Office of Military Student Services for all their support.

Silouan Green, you are an amazing person and inspiration for creating a remarkable workbook to help others. Without your workbook, our book would not have been possible. Our writing has helped us heal in immeasurable ways.

And most of all, thank you to all the members of The Ladder UPP™ group, past and present who were there through thick and thin, supporting each other all the way.

Contents

Healing Words

What an honor to be a part of this incredible anthology of hope. "Healing Words" could not be a more apt title for the power of unlocking our inner hopes, dreams, demons, trauma, and all the rest of life's tragically beautiful experiences.

It seems just yesterday that I was asked if the Ladder UPP™ would be a good tool for using in a student writing group at IPFW by Jo Vaughan, the Director of Military Student Services. I enthusiastically said yes as I simultaneously reflected on some of the trauma writing had helped me overcome - PTSD, depression, and suicide. To see my pain turned into something positive that helps others is an incredibly therapeutic and life affirming revelation.

That is the power of healing words. They change our perspective. They make us realize that regardless of what tragedies may have befallen us, whatever bad decision we might have made, we always have a choice in how we respond. Will we move forward, or will we wallow in a past that we cannot change?

I applaud all of those who have contributed to this wonderful work, "Healing Words." You are torches that proclaim it is healthy to realize suffering is as much a part of life as the joys, and when we use our suffering as fuel for life, all of our experiences, good and bad, become a beacon of hope.

Sincerely, Silouan Green

Dedication

To those who have been in our shoes, experiencing trauma and memories.

You are not alone.

Airport and Travel Mysteries

This was written following a long layover in a major airline hub. I love to observe people and their behavior, interactions, and how their relationships are manifested in the best of times and in the worst of times. Airline travel just happens to enable folks to demonstrate the worst of themselves quite often and in great contrast to those who choose a higher road.

-J. Vaughan

Airport and Travel Mysteries

Airports provide some amazing opportunities for people observation. Chicago O'Hare is no exception! Some of the characters were happy, some sad, some wearing looks of utter bewilderment, and some were downright ominous.

I felt sorry for the middle-aged couple who were dressed in business casual, seated close side-by-side, but totally engrossed in their individual cell phones. They were missing some great quality time while wearing out their fingerprints.

The large concourse held over thirty gates for flight departures. Folks milled about, some frantically in full searching for the right gate, while others sprawled about the seating area with their numerous belongings strewn about them in disarray.

One poor soul ran up to a gate, took one look at the monitor that stated the flight had departed, whereupon she promptly threw her bags down on the floor with loud cursing. She spoke briefly with the staff at the counter, then walked over to a wall and dropped to the floor, wailing like a banshee. Everyone looked in her direction and security stepped in to escort her from the area. I prayed for her to find a positive solution to her dilemma.

The Rastafarian guy in full African design and colors in his knitted cap and jacket, the football jock, the baseball player, and the elderly woman accompanied by her son, all in contrast with the Asian gentleman who was laughing while chasing a toddler - who even though wearing a leash, had escaped the tether and was running in full gales of laughter. The man finally put on a burst of speed and caught the child. They both collapsed on the carpet in a mass of giggles. There was a "distinguished" gentleman who arrived in check-in just in time to board the plane with the elite first class pass-holders. Plugged in to his cellphone via ear buds, he kept a running conversation online while expecting the airline staff to know when he was addressing them versus the caller. (I found this a bit absurd.)

One gentleman wandered around aimlessly while telling someone on his cell phone that "Lexi passed away...." He was dressed in a suit and a female was also wandering around within a five-foot circle of space that bubbled around him. Both the male and woman appeared to be operating in a fog of disbelief with a clearly damaged cognitive system.

Two Chinese women were comparing their boarding passes and arguing about what was typed on the pass. Another young woman who had recently disembarked from a plane heard them and went over to explain the group numbers for boarding.

A wide variety of personalities showed up to man the ticket desks. Pilots, service attendants, custodial staff, agents, and flight attendants took turns punching the keyboard and running large amounts of data on printouts, keys dangling like holsters on hips and pockets.

I saw a couple of families with small children; two had strollers, backpacks, blankets and a plethora of stuffed animals. One of the families appeared to be a refugee family - a little dazed and confused, but quickly moving toward a group of American workers who were waiting to meet them.

The shuttle van driver was an interesting black African man, aged 65, who had been working in the service industry since his early twenties. We talked about the pressures of concierge work and some of the interesting personalities and celebrities we had had the privilege to meet in person. His most famous person was Marlene Dietrich - he was her personal driver while she was performing in a small theatre late in her life, as she was in her eighties.

This short-lived conversation we shared was an actual connection between two highly disparate people divided by race, gender, geography, and culture, who were still able to completely understand each other's contribution. The conversation was honored by a warm handshake and expressions of gratitude for the shared friendly acceptance as we went on our separate ways.

Call Her Veteran

-Denise K. Buhr

Veterans' Day Flag Ceremony 2013
Indiana University-Purdue University Fort Wayne

Call Her Veteran

WAC

Warrior

Hello Girl

GI Jane

Lioness

Angel

She has been called many names; some unspeakable.

Call her one more:

Veteran

They are the unlikeliest women.

You cannot tell by looking at them.

They work in the next cubicle,

Get coffee at the corner shop,

Live on your block,

Lead ordinary or extraordinary lives.

Over two million strong.

Yes, strong.

Women. Veterans.

Not the flawed or fragmented images of popular culture;

Not novelties, anomalies, jokes.

But strong, proud

Veterans

Women

Who purposely sought the opportunity

and proudly fulfilled a self-made obligation.

They were not bound by law,

But they heard and answered the call

To serve their country;

Our country

Today's military woman

stands on the shoulders of generations before her.

Women who,

for patriotism, pride, a purpose in life;

for adventure, action, a chance to advance;

for escape, education, and every reason in between,
solemnly swore to support and defend,
to bear true faith and allegiance,
and to obey orders,
"so help me God."
She has dressed in men's breeches to blend in
And buried her femininity under fifty pounds of combat
gear.
She has served behind the lines and as "boots on the
ground,"
Beside the men and beyond expectation.
Brass said she shouldn't;
Young men said she couldn't;
Old ones retired in their Posts said she didn't;
"She's not one of us."
She is a woman.
She will always be a woman.
She is not one of "the guys."
They are not the same.
But they take the same oath;
They wear the same uniform;
They defend the same country.
From cook and clerk and player in the band
To gunner and pilot and the highest levels of command,
She *has* "done it" and done it well;
Served with honor and dedication.
They seek no medals or special distinctions,
Just your understanding that
They are women,
They too are veterans.

Applebee's

My best friend and I had been through some trouble days without sleep. This was our treat! There is good somewhere in life.
        -Dawn Cunningham

Applebee's

The day starts early in the morning, with the bed not yet slept in—for either gal who had walked into the restaurant. Applebee's® salad dishes sit upon a table, empty, while the two gals await the desert that consists of three scoops of ice cream upon a large chocolate-chip cookie with whip cream piled in swirls around the stack and each pile decorated with crushed Oreos— the whole dish crisscrossed and swirled with chocolate syrup. Little is said between the two.

It doesn't matter if any words are said, the night hasn't ended and they are meeting the new day in style. The desert comes. If it was true that eyes could pop out of your head, theirs would. Together "Oh my" escapes, and the older adds, "We won't be able to eat this all." They each dip a spoon into the fluff first, smiling, moaning as women sexually charged. Each scoop is savored until a serving is left. Each have eaten a serving and a half. They can go no further. They are filled, delighted, perked for the long morning before their heads hit the pillow.

Massawa Beach

My military service took me to the east coast of Africa in the 1950s. It was an accompanied tour, which meant that my family was also with me. There were other American families and some single military stations on top of a mountain just short of a mile high. Occasionally, we would go down the mountain, across the desert, past the salt mines, and to the Massawa beach on the Red Sea.

-Jack Hannigan

Massawa Beach

On Friday, we left the mountain in the mid-afternoon, my family joined two other families and once again took the trip to the beach. We planned to stay the weekend and return home Sunday before 6:00 p.m., when the road closed for the night. We took tents, food, coolers, and play things for the children. Upon arrival, the males set up two tents on the beach, one for the women and one for the children to keep in the shade. They started a fire in the sand for cooking our evening meal. Then we opened the cooler, had a beer, and relaxed for a while.

The women and children had already gotten their swimsuits on and were playing in the water of the Red Sea. We changed into our swimsuits and joined the families in the water. Our attire for the weekend was bare feet and swimsuits. We all got out of the water and the women started cooking the evening meal. After eating, the children were bedded down. The adults lay in the sand, watching the sun set in the west. When it was time for bed, the women went into the tent and the guys roughed it on the sandy beach.

The sun comes up in the east early, and we were all awake by seven. Each family went about getting ready for a new day; breakfast, relaxing, and playing with children. About mid-morning we heard a noise in the distance. We went over the sand dune and saw people and a camel train heading our way, stopping about fifty yards from us. We realized that it was a nomadic group wandering the desert. They set up camp and bedded down the camels.

Around noon, we were getting lunch ready. The nomads came over the sand dune and rushed for the water with their clothing on. After a short swim, they took off their clothes and lay them out to dry on the hot sand. There they were in the nude; women, men, and children. Then they returned to the warm waters of the Red Sea.

We looked at them and herded the children into their tent. When the nomads saw this, they started to laugh at us with our swimsuits on. This was their custom, how they washed and dried their clothing and how they cleansed their bodies. A short time later, they all got out of the water, picked up their dry clothing and got dressed, then returned to their campsite.

The rest of Saturday went by and we had our time and fun at the beach. The nomads never came back over to go swimming. Saturday night, as we were settling down for sleeping, we could hear the nomads in their camp.

Sunday morning, once again the sun rose early. We prepared breakfast and realized that we could not hear the nomads. We discovered that they had gotten up before sunrise and travelled off to another part of the desert. We all enjoyed our last swim in the Red Sea, packed up, and headed back up the mountain to our homes.

If I Could Fly

I wrote this poem not long after my mother completed suicide. We were given a prompt from The Ladder Upp™ workbook, called "If I Could Fly," where we would continue the sentence and write about it. All I could think of if I had the power to fly, I would visit my mother.

-ML Wissing

If I Could Fly

If I could fly
So way up high
Above the clouds
And touch the sky

I'd spread my wings
A song I'd sing
And fly above
The awful things

I'd laugh out loud
Mom, you'd be so proud
Make my home
On a fluffy cloud

Be no more tears
Nothing of fear
As long as I
Was flying here

Sit by the gate
For you I'd wait
Visiting hours
That never close late

We'd hug and sigh
Not tears in our eyes
We'd never have to say goodbye

. . . If I could fly.

"The group has given me an outlook to express without fear. It has given me hope that I will get better. It has showed me how to pay attention to find the triggers. We help each other, regardless where we stand in life. When hope feels distant, the group brings light, even when discussing the bad. The [The Ladder UPP™ Workbook] book is a guidance in finding a path that works for me.

- Dawn Cunningham

If I Could Fly

- Denise K. Buhr

"The sky starts at your feet. Think how brave you are to walk around." - Anne Herbert

If I Could Fly

If I could fly
I'd wing my way over
traffic, construction,
ice and snow.
I'd never have a
flat tire, dead battery,
or worry the gas tank was low.
I'd leave behind the noise:
horns blasting,
music throbbing,
private conversations – not so,
the racing, the roaring,
rage pouring on the roadways,
hell-bent on getting
wherever they must go.

I'd stretch out my arms,
wiggle my toes,
lift my eyes to the sky
and floating up I'd fly away;
rising above the din
of traffic on roads
that stretch beyond the horizon,
ribbons of black and gray;
sailing past crowds of people,
and the bricks and boards
of houses large and little,
offices, businesses, stores.

I'd soar into quiet space
and make my own path
up and down,
straight or curved,
where only winged creatures

are allowed to roam,
creating paths that
cross and merge
but never interfere with mine.
Free to go wherever
mind and spirit will,
to clouds, to stars, beyond forever.

Or I'd float silently
to where the ground is verdant,
the beaches bare,
the ocean a color only God could mix.
I'd softly slide in,
my toes digging into the sand,
and I'd lay myself down
to let go of the ickiness.
Soft pillows in a blanket of blue,
a sandy bed of soothing heat,
scents and colors of infinite delicacy,
the lullaby of the moving deep.
When within is refreshed and quiet
and the longing to escape grows
silent in the stillness of peace,
I'll fly away home.

Dark Dressing

Hyper-vigilance or situation awareness is often thought of as simple to "fix" and only those who live with it, on a daily basis truly understand. No matter if it is the service member or the spouse, both will still live with the consequences.

This is in response to a workbook assignment to write about a negative memory, or a recurrent trigger. Somewhat fictionalized, this story describes the pain of futile effort to master the unchangeable.
- J. Vaughan

Dark Dressing

The alarm was supposed to ring with pleasant music but at 0500, there just isn't any kind of music that is pleasant to hear. Marley reached out automatically to silence it and thought for a moment that she could maybe re-set it for another hour later and go back to sleep but just as quickly realized that was a "no go" and slumped back into the pillow-her blood pressure rising in anger before her eyes were even open. Furiously, she threw her legs out of the covers in a rush, grabbed her clothes off the dresser and her books to begin the "Mad (emphasis furious) Hatter" tip-toe dance of getting ready for work trying to avoid making any sound that would trigger a PTSD response from the figure still asleep under the tangle of blankets. The days of snuggling together under the covers and waking gently to a loving embrace, had disappeared since his deployment and hadn't made an appearance since his return home.

Marley pulled the bedroom door closed, very gently turning the knob just so quietly -- *How much noise does a toilet have to make to make when the flush mechanism pours water from the tank into the bowl? Would it help to drown out the noise if the radio was on, or would that just make it worse?* Not wanting to turn on too many lights (another huge no-no) Marley slinked on tiptoes into the kitchen to make her breakfast. Coffee is a must, then search for something quick, easy, and nourishing to gobble while standing over the sink, putting the percolator together by very. gently picking up each piece of the mechanism like the game "Pick Up Sticks", not disturbing one piece with another, setting them soundlessly on the counter while filling the pot with water, then again ever so gently adding each piece, moving in stealth-mode in the dark from cupboard to sink with the filter and coffee until the pot is assembled and plugged in. Breathe!

On stealth-toes, Marley returned to the bathroom, "Why is the bathroom so close to the bedroom?" Cat-burglar style, she opened the door, held the knob until the latch met the catch, turning softly, the latch catches in silence. Some folks sing in the shower, but Marley notices how loud the sound of water is as it slides down her hair and gathers at the drain. "Please don't let me drop the shampoo bottle, or "God-forbid" the basket of bath brushes, soaps, and moisturizers. The towel is blissfully quiet as she wraps herself in its warmth and gently ever so quietly brushes the water from her skin. Breathing almost normally now, Marley glances at her reflection in the mirror and wonders where that young girl went who used to live in her body.

Dressing in the walk-in closet, Marley doesn't even turn on that light, rather she holds a small LED flashlight in her mouth, she dresses as quickly, silently as possible, making certain that the flashlight only shines on the actual clothes illuminating only the color and front/back of the shirt and pants. Suddenly her brain flashes to an image of how silly she must look standing on one leg like a flamingo in the dark, flashlight in mouth, getting dressed while he is snoring a few feet away, oblivious to the effort she was making this pitch dark morning, as she did everyday. Marley's mind becomes a freight train runaway as it explodes with her thoughts racing, ordering herself to escape:

"I can't control the laughter!"
"I have to. . .Get. .. OUT!
"Oh Crap! Don't make a single sound!"

Marley ran on stealth-tiptoes to the next room, where she fell in a heap on the floor, arms wrapped around knees and head. The giggles changed from laughter to big tear drops rolling down her cheeks as she grieved for the pretzel-positioned woman who was sitting like a broken child on the floor, weeping because the inner child knows she is slowly dying to self and the joy light of her life is waning like the feeble light of a candle being blown out. Perhaps peace will come with the darkness. Perhaps not.

Salt Production

During my tour in the military in Eritrea and Ethiopia, the family would go down the mountain and across the desert to the Port of Massawa, Eritrea for rest and relaxation. I found it interesting to see the local populous producing salt for sale on the local market and for transport to other parts of East Africa.
-John D. Hannigan

Salt Production

The local populace made a simple process of producing salt from the salt water from the Red Sea. Initially they would dig a square hole in the sand 20-foot-long, 20-foot-wide, by 1-foot deep. This was known as a salt bed. Then the populace would pump water from the Red Sea and fill the salt bed. The heat in the desert was on the average of 120 degrees and the salt water would evaporate, leaving the salt for harvest.

Both Nomad tribes that roamed the desert and the local populace would then work the salt bed and harvest the salt. The salt would be four to six inches thick. They would then cut the salt into blocks. They used camels to transport the salt to other East African locations. The camels had harnesses that the salt was put in.

The nomad tribes would then lead the camels on their trip along the East Coast of Africa. The salt was their purchasing power for the tribe and the Queen of the nomads. The nomads would traverse the desert area, selling salt wherever they decided to stop and visit. They traveled through Eritrea, Ethiopia, and Somalia. The nomad tribes of East Africa did not recognize paper money. They would only accept coins. They bartered for beer, pop cans and bottles, or anything else that they could use in traveling.

On their return trip across the desert, they would once again stop at the salt beds and process salt as they continued their wandering of the desert. Salt was the commodity the nomad tribes and the local populace lived off of to provide the necessary income for their Tribes and families.

My family found it interesting to see how a simple process of making salt from the Red Sea salt water could provide an economy for local populace and nomad tribes to make a living and raise their families.

It Must Be Rain

I couldn't pass up the change of writing about a moment that was loving and humorous. Little children are very perceptive; we only need to listen.
- Dawn Cunningham

It Must Be Rain

For two weeks, the shower has been broken. Baths have become a cuss word. On a Tuesday, the eldest son, David, buys all the replacement parts. By evening, the
shower head is working, the hand-held shower piece is flowing once again. The first to step in is Aunt Ginny. In the living room stands Will, David's son, only son, listening closely with head cocked and a curious look as his Mammaw walks out of the bathroom. One word explodes as his finger points, and he quickly steps to the closing bathroom door: "Shouw-er, shouw-er."

Mammaw scoops him up, saying, "Yes, shower. The shower is fixed."

The water sounds like the trickling rain just before the storm. Once Mammaw sits him onto the couch, he is up again pointing, "Shouw-er, shouw-er," grabbing his Mammaw's fingers, pulling her along to the bathroom door, where he pushes open the cracked door.

"Yes, Auntie is taking a shower." However, Will keeps insisting, while climbing upon the toilet to stand on the lid, "Shouw-er, shouw-er."

"No, you can't take a shower now; Auntie is in there," Mammaw speaks as softly as possible and loud enough to be heard over the shower. The pikes creak. The shower curtain slowly pulls back a bit, a head appearing with wet dripping hair, "Do Will want a shower."

"Shouw-er, shouw-er," he points. The words repeating.

"You take a shower with Auntie," Ginny smiles.

Will quickly slides off the top of the toilet, dancing, "Shouw-er, shouw-er," his feet bouncing in delight, "Shouw-er, shouw-er."

"Alright, let's take off your diaper," Mammaw reaches down, realizing before it is too late, to find he might be a little more than pissy. He is moving for the tub, ready to climb in; Mammaw pull him back, "Wait Will, we
have to take care of that diaper."

Mammaw takes the diaper off slowly, seeing the full diaper isn't as bad as she thought. "Okay, Will," she lifts him into the tub as he pushes back the shower curtain, giggling with joy:

"RAIN!"

The Ladder UPP™ has been a fantastic group for me to express myself in writing, and to get support. On bad days, I never feel alone, but surrounded by people who understand what I am going through, who never blame me for feeling what I am feeling, and make me laugh. Without them, I don't know where I would be today.
-ML Wissing

Holes in Their Soles

- Denise K. Buhr

". . . it's not so much about the shoes, but the person wearing them." - Adriana Trigiani

"What a wonderful beautiful thing, to wiggle your toes."
- Dalton Trumbo

August 6 is Wiggle Your Toes Day.

Holes in Their Soles

Johnny had big feet. Jenny had little. Marcus and Maggie and Samuel and Sue had feet somewhere in the middle. But they all had holes in the soles of their shoes.

Johnny went to the cobbler to see if he could put on a patch. The cobbler said, "The hole is too big," and then he just laughed.

Jenny went to the store. She wanted to buy a new pair. The clerk said, "Baby feet don't need shoes. Now get out of here!"

Marcus and Maggie wanted boots to keep out the wet and cold. But all they could find was a left one for him and a right one for her and both had holes in their soles.

Samuel and Sue tried cardboard and glue but that made a messy goo. Then they used string to tie on flattened cans but that was slippery and slick and they had to "walk" home on their knees and their hands.

One day Johnny and Jenny and Marcus and Maggie and Samuel and Sue decided to take off their shoes. They threw away their socks too. And they said, "Our feet have soles and they *don't* have holes. Our feet are sweet, our feet are grand, upon our feet we stand. We don't need shoes with holes in their soles. And without them our toes are free!"

They left their shoes by the door and off they went to explore. They squished their toes in garden mud after soft spring rains and turned them brown with dusty ground from fields now planted with grain. Under summer's sun, they buried their toes in warm sand and cooled them at the water's edge. They wriggled them in soft green grass and plucked dandelions with them under the hedge. They kicked up autumn leaves and crunched them down with their tough toes and calloused soles, then warmed their feet by the fire. But winter snows were too much for their toes. Though it was not their desire, they tried to put on those old, hole-y shoes. But their feet had grown, just a bit, and now were too big to fit.

When Johnny and Jenny and Marcus and Maggie and Samuel and Sue had shoes - even shoes with holes in their soles - there was so much they could do. They could go school, learn the times two and the Golden Rule, and why pigs *oink* and cows *moo*. They could go to a show, sit in the back row to boo the villain and cheer the beautiful girl's beau. They were welcomed at diners, if they had the dough, where they could get a meat and two veg with a slice of bread or even a fancy dinner roll. Shopkeepers said hello and took their pennies for bubble gum to blow, balls to throw, tiny toys to tow, and pretty buttons to sew. All because they had shoes, even if those shoes had holes in the soles. But now, NO! "No shirt, no shoes, no service!"

So Johnny and Jenny and Marcus and Maggie and Samuel and Sue left that old town for greener pastures and new skies of blue. How far they walked, no one knew. One day they met an old woman on the road coming from the market. She asked why their faces were so sad and darkened, and listened to their tale of woe. She was round and wrinkled and not very tall. She wore a gown of colored patches. Her face was kind, her eyes twinkled, and she had a smile for all. She opened her basket - oh, what a feast! - and fed them bread and jam, cheese and ham, and cherries and berries and cream. Then she opened her heart instead of saying "adieu" and invited them home where the old woman lived . . . in a shoe!

It was actually a boot, all leathery brown, with the smokestack thirty feet from the ground. There was a door in the heel on either side and windows galore to let in the light. The laces were staircases to get to the top, where just under the peak there was a small spot perfect for watching sunsets and moonrises and meteor streaks.

They helped her in the garden and she taught them about plants. They fixed the roof and painted the doors and she patched their torn pants. She showed them how to be kind to all living things and they brought her stray kittens, found treasures, and dandelion rings. She cooked them good things to eat, savory and sweet, and they made her laugh with delight. They gave her hugs every morning and she kissed them to bed each night.

Now Johnny and Jenny and Marcus and Maggie and Samuel and Sue still went barefoot three seasons of the year. But when the winds turned cold and it began to snow, at the foot of their beds, new shoes would appear. And one thing more that made wearing shoes less of a chore - new socks in all the right hues knitted by the old woman who lived in the shoe. Johnny got purple ones crisscrossed with gold. Jenny's were bright pink adorned with flowers so bold. Marcus wore candy-striped ones that reached his knees and Maggie had checked ones in oranges and greens. Samuel's were yellow and fit like gloves just so, with little pockets for each of his toes. And Sue liked blue because it sounded the same as her name. But not just any blue would do - only blue of the sky when the summer is new.

Johnny still had big feet. Jenny still had little. Marcus and Maggie and Samuel and Sue still had feet somewhere in the middle. But in the old woman's shoe, the only hole in that sole was the root cellar, a room snug and clean, where all the vegetables and fruits were kept for when days were dark and lean. And whether they wore shoes or would choose not to, love filled the holes in their *souls*.

Overheard Comments: A Found Poem

In February 2015, we did an assignment in *The Ladder UPP™ Workbook* by Silouan Green, where we paid attention to things said around us, writing them down, and bringing them to our next meeting. These statements, heard around the college campus, became a collaborated "found" poem.

Contributors:
J. Vaughan
Denise K. Buhr
Dawn Cunningham

Overheard Comments: A Found Poem

Car 1, 45. Car 2, 447.
Rrrrrrrrrrrrrrrrrrrrrrrrr!
Sometimes . . . oh, it's so cold it's hard to speak.
That's all you get.
Noooo, ah-ah.
I thought it was a dog in the hallway barking and
coming to get us!
After we go over . . . .
Nobody warned me.
I don't know what to tell you, but I can't take care of
this for you.
I can't leave; I'm in class . . . well, heading to class.
Will they let me in the class with this thing on my head?
I have to get her some pink shoes.
Here are a few samples I gathered this morning.
I thought you gave up beer for Lent . . .
Make it instant.
Thanks Man, you're great.
Whoo hoo! He did it again!
Having fun are we? I hope so!
Whoa, Ky! Stop!
No! No! Don't stop me!
I have a question for ya . . .
I know it's not the save button!
Haha, you're so funny!
Read this.
Cold! Come on Jack.
Wow! It is cold out there today!
Happy humming in the restroom.

Humor Lesson/Story

I love humor, it helps me to deal with the everyday grieving over losses, bad decisions, and wrong paths taken. Choosing to be happy in spite of circumstances takes effort, and sometimes the effort involves the ridiculous, and writing about it is enormously cathartic.
  -J. Vaughan

Humor Lesson/Story

There are lots of stories about women, stories about how saintly they are, how sweet, how gorgeous, such terrific mothers, cooks, wives, etc. This is not that kind of story. This is a story about a real, ordinary crazy lady who sometimes just couldn't get it together if "IT" was swept up in a dustpan and dumped in a basket.

This lady had some issues, some were with health, some with mental health, some with all the other things of the world that just get in the way of being happy and whatever normal means today.

She did try to get enough sleep; she set her alarm for 7-8 hours beyond bedtime, which was the first in a series of mishaps, fundamental craziness, and downright frustration. Getting seven hours of sleep in one night, requires that the person actually falls asleep, and soon after retiring, but NO-o-o-o-oo-o-not so fast! After tossing and turning until 1:30 a.m., she throws back the blankets, vaults out of the bed to "quietly" slip into the bathroom before heading to the living room to read for a while.

Unfortunately, she doesn't see well at night, and the nightlight just isn't bright enough, and well, there is a WALL by the bedroom door, and ANOTHER WALL by the bathroom door, and they sort of just jumped out at her and of course she smack dab full force slammed her face into not one, but both walls, in her ricochet to the toilet. Cursing like a mute sailor, she stumbles to the facility and makes a grand gesture to normalcy thinking all is now well- not so fast. . . the toilet paper roll now decides to spring from the holder onto the floor, roll past the bathtub and under the sink. *What to do, what to do.*

Shaking drips as best she can, she then reaches, stretches oh so far, but nope, gotta make a stand. *UGH!* Ok got the roll, got cleaned up, and then, oh joy the flush mechanism is over-extended and the flushing will not stop. Jiggle the handle, open the tank, fiddle with the flapper at the bottom of the tank. Finally the flushing stops – toity was never so clean.

Deciding that she needs to shower before relaxing in the living room, and no sleepiness in sight, she thinks a shower in warm water will help her to relax and fall asleep. She knew naught about the dime-sized bit of soap bar on the floor of the tub, a hidden missile of terrorism about to sabotage her in the worse way.

She did manage to get all soaped up, hair washed, conditioner on her hair, and then, the attack! Yup, all full force slippage began its ricochet of her body first to the floor of the tub, then the sides, back to the floor, into the glass shower doors, all the while flailing and yelling and bumping all manner of body parts with her full weight engaged. One may have believed that the raucous slamming of body parts against the wall of the shower, the tub floor, and the shower door would have woken the dead, but not her hubby, and not the cats.

After much tumbling around, she finally managed to sit on the floor of the tub, allowed the water to pound down on her head while she gathered her senses and then she gingerly picked herself up and crawled out, embarrassed, bruised, and exhausted onto the throw rug. Drying herself on the first towel she get her fingers on, she silently prays it isn't the one she used to wipe up the floor with earlier.

Peeping into the bedroom, she sees that she has not caused anyone else to lose a wink of sleep. Now the decision: go back to bed, or do some reading –she opts to crawl back under the covers and lays sleepless until the light begins to bleed through the blinds and begrudgingly gets back out of bed, remembering that the WALLS are still there, and bumps her way as though in a pinball machine all the way to the kitchen.

Now coffee sounds like a great idea. Unfortunately, no, it's not. The water heats to boiling, the coffee grounds are in the pour-over filter, and then the fun begins. Have you ever seen 5 scoops of coffee newly wet and slushy from boiled water when it dumps over onto the counter, the cupboard, and the floor? Yup, café au mess! Grabbing a cloth she begins mopping up the mess only to see that she now needs another shower because the coffee slush has managed to cover her feet and arms and now is also on her face.

Dilemma, to shower again, *hmm no*, because the bruise on her hip is now turning a distinct black, not blue, and the size of the bruise exceeds a normal tea towel. Mopping up, no coffee to drink, she opts to make a jar of protein powder and milk shake. That would require the lid of the jar to be on tight enough not to leak. . . yup, you guessed it, first shake of the jar and milk, protein powder, and gobs of nearly mixed goop go flying all over the kitchen.

Stupefied, she stands transfixed, daring not to breathe, afraid that any movement on her part will create more slop. Oh goody, the cats are awake, just in time to start tracking the slopped coffee grounds all over the kitchen floor. Not one, not two, but three cats in coffee slush on the creamy white tile floor.

She tosses the jar into the sink, mops up the mess, and the floor, feeds the cats, and goes back to the bathroom. Starting over, she turns on the shower faucet, carefully climbs in, sits on the floor, and lets the water wash the coffee slushy off her, and then carefully climbs back out. It is now full daylight, she is an hour late leaving for work, and decides right then and there that it is a "sick day" and goes back to bed.

Her hubby now wakes up, walks in perfect stealth to the kitchen and sees the aftermath of coffee Armageddon. He walks back to the bedroom, sees his wife still in bed, and says: "Honey, are you ok, are you ill?"

"Yup, I'm sick as a dog and I ain't movin' from this bed!"

"Umm ok, where is the coffee?"

She throws the pillow at him and pulls the blankets over her head while muttering swear words in a steady stream of mumble.
Epilogue:
Later that evening her husband sees the glorious bruise of all bruises on her hip and leg and wants to know who did that to her. She takes him by the hand and delivers him to the shower.

The Road

Roads are similar to life. Twists, turns, bumps, breaks, curbs, shoulders, no shoulders, dirty gravel and concrete. Each is met over a journey to our final destinations. 525,600 minutes in a year. 525,600 steps. Walk, don't run.
  -ML Wissing

The Road

As I walk down the endless road,
I watch as I feet stop before a line drawn
across the hard, sometimes broken blacktop.

Another line.

It took me a year to get from the last one to this one.
525,600 steps.
The same distance from the line before that.
And the line before that.
Not that anyone counts them.
Not that anyone notices.

I take a moment to stop, and look behind me.
A moment of reflection.
A moment to see just how far I had come in this past
year.
See what I've done.

The road lay stretched behind me as far as the eye could
see.
Sometimes broken, sometimes smooth.
But I had gotten through.
Somehow, I had survived everything I was thrown in my
direction.

I look back at my feet.
Another line.
Another year.
Another chance for improvement.
For failure.
For laughter.
For tears.

I take a breath and let it out.
And step over the line.
I begin my journey once more.
525,600 more steps to go.

Happy new year.

Blinking Lights

After many nights of not sleeping, the mind begins to see and hear things that don't exist. It made for a good storyline.
- Dawn Cunningham

Blinking Lights

Two minutes of twelve. The numbers glow like two anonymous cat eyes. The wave of light flows even and noticeable. A blink here, a blink there, and still the slow iridescence red caresses the air.

I couldn't sleep, not tonight, not the night before, or before that, not since all my lights came on at once at twelve midnight. The first time it happened was during a thunderstorm. The odd thing about it they never went off. I had to go around to each room and flip the switches four times - on, off, on, off. The following night I did the same, and when I had finished my travels they all came on again! Now, I lie in bed and watch the lights come on, go off, in rhythm or hazardously, all together or half at a time. My whole house is a light show from twelve midnight to one. There is no sleeping for me, or my neighbor, who tells me strange noises leak from my basement and cling to the trees and shrubs, and to the side of his house - even after all is quiet in my house. Why doesn't he just call the police so they can come and see it too? Prove that I'm not nuts; prove that it isn't me doing it? There's one problem with his report. I don't hear the moans and screams, the chirping and chattering. He thinks I have a band playing and exotic dancers in my basement every night. Is he nuts?

The Tale of the Naugahyde

There is a species of reptilian animal that roams the South Californian desert called the Naugahyde. The population is now around a thousand and the species is diminishing daily as the young ones are killed for their skins. Recently, the Department of the Interior has placed this animal on the endangered species list.
-John D. Hannigan

The Tale of the Naugahyde

The Naugahyde is a small reptile about 12 to 15 inches long. Its skin is considered rare because of its soft texture.

A friend asked if it was a Native American name. I guess there could have been a reptile that was named Naugahyde by the Southwest Native Americans in days gone past. Folklore says that they used to kill them so they could make moccasins to cover their feet because the skin was so soft.

Another friend said that there was furniture and upholstery called Naugahyde. I guess there could be, since the soft reptilian skin could be woven with other materials to make a comfortable surface to sit on.

I suppose that also, someone could make belts, shoes, or handbags out of the soft skin as well.

We, at the Save the Naugahyde Foundation, hope that you will partake of our goal and donate to the foundation so that the Naugahyde can be preserved and the population increased, thereby being taken off the Department of the Interior's endangered species list.

Worth Fighting For

I think somewhere in my past, my inner spirit decided that enough was enough and the option of remaining a victim was not for me. As I have struggled with domestic violence and violation throughout my life, I have learned not only the "British stiff upper lip," but the tough fist of being a warrior woman. Never, never again, will I be a victim – beware the recompense for those who may consider the attempt to place me there.
  -J. Vaughan

Worth Fighting For

Hmmm, maybe I have a pugilistic bent in my character, or perhaps I just value a plethora of causes, people, and situations. Narrowing down my choices for which I would fight, is next to impossible. Prioritization of most valued is tough, as that effort requires that I define my fighting posture. My fighting stance is not standing legs at shoulder width, fists pumped in the air, but my favorite and most effective fighting stance—on my knees before God.

How is that a fighting stance? Spiritual warfare is no joke and I have been called into active duty for several years. Like a heavily trained mercenary, I take up the fight for those who may not even be aware that I am battling for them, engaging in warfare that threatens life and limb, body and soul. *Prayer Warrior* is a calling not a choice, a gift assignment that costs the recipient hours of sleep, restful peace, and a willingness to engage battle even though the time of waging war comes when it is least expected. A persistent nudging wakens me in the night, stops me midday with an urgent message, or re-directs a personal prayer time to focus on a specific need thrust into my presence.

I am willing to fight for my beliefs, my rights, my life, my family, and my friends. That may translate to fighting for folks I've never met, when called upon to do so by the Highest Power. The first thing as a mom that comes to mind, is of course my children. That mother instinct rises strong in me and should one of my babies, though grown adults, face a trial or tribulation, I am in fighting stance. My physical fighting stance generally requires armament and that is covered with hardware accompanied by projectile objects, baseball bats, etc. which is only called upon in situations of imminent physical attack.

Other things in life, would have to be considered on a case by case basis. I have experienced a wide variety of "traumas" in my life and those experiences have taught me that many worldly issues or things simply don't matter in the grand scheme of life. "Don't sweat the small stuff, and it is all small stuff" is an attitude that gives me the grace to avoid worry, fear, and anxiety. I've learned a lot of patience through the past 6 plus decades and know that I know that I know life is for the living - and living every minute to the fullest is my ultimate goal.

I don't often quote my mother, but one phrase she used to say nearly every day: *"CAN'T is too lazy and stubborn to try!"* Giving up was never an option, and frustration was not allowed to be expressed. From her I learned that hard work was the ultimate overcomer strategy and to this day, when I have to choose between fighting about some idiotic annoyance or ideology, I choose to become busy with ordinary tasks that must and should be done, and I do them with excellence to give myself the time and space to make the decision as to how I will engage in the battle or leave it entirely.

There is no shame in failure, only in the absence of "trying." So I pick myself up by my bootstraps and I try again to move forward even if that means standing in the face of fierce battle, whether it be physical, mental or spiritual, and thereby create my own boundary of battle zone and I choose my weapons carefully. Never underestimate your enemy, especially if your enemy is *moi*!

WHAT HAS THE LADDER UPP "DONE FOR YOU?

When I was asked to be a facilitator for this writing group, I was honored. I may not have PTSD but I do know that if you are alive, you have stress! And if you live long enough, you'll eventually encounter something that shakes up, maybe even shatters your world. When I was diagnosed with breast cancer, I couldn't think about much else; so I wrote a fictionalized account of my experiences. And it became a prize-winning play. That's what this group is all about: to use the power of writing for help and healing.

One of the caveats of this group is that nothing we write is good or bad. There's no judgement or evaluation, only observation – what do we, the readers and/or listeners, see and understand in another's work. Or in the words of Marine Brigadier General Angela Salinas, "I know what I said; now tell me what you heard." So we write, we read and listen, we comment, we write some more, we share, we re-write, and then we do it all again. And again. And somewhere along the way, if it works the way we hope, we become better writers and a little more whole.
*   - Denise K. Buhr*

Silence is Loud When Words Are Kept

As always, I am writing about the silence and oppression with poetry. Each time I write about silence and oppression, it gives me more courage. This poem was brought on by my willingness to not speak out but found its way through my writing.
- Dawn Cunningham

Silence is Loud When Words Are Kept

no words are lain
on the ground, not even
a letter to plant a root
where have all the words
been kept; where are they
all stored?

face-filed in rows unsown,
lips cracked and parched; no watering can
filled to feed the tongue tied
by loneliness, by quietness, by oppression
deemed depression.

Survivor's Tale

I'd written this while sitting on my cot in Iraq in 2004. We had just experienced the worst mortar attack in our deployment, and my best friend's roommate had been killed.

It was the first casualty that I had personally known, the first real brush of death, the first startling realization that any of us could be next, even me.
-ML Wissing

Survivor's Tale

The scariest sound I've ever heard
Was hearing my heart beating.
The worse pain I've ever felt
Was taking in air to breathe.
The more horrible thing I've ever seen
Was looking back at me in the mirror.
Nothing seems the same anymore,
Nothing will be the same.
For I've done the unthinkable,
The unimaginable.

I survived.

I'm still here.
This isn't Darwin's Theory,
Survival of the Fittest.
This isn't "Survivor" or "Big Brother".
This is reality.
The drama known as Life.
Showing seven days a week,
Twenty-four hours a day.
We're built to survive,
We've learned to strive to win.
But did anyone notice,
If you survive,
You still lose?

Collections

As a Senior Citizen suffering with PTSD, I took time to look back and review all the collections and pen pals that I had as a child. That memory led me through my lifetime where those collections and pen pals were no longer there. At my current age, our society in the United States has become a disposable society. Collections and pen pals are no longer present only a memory.

-John D. Hannigan

Collections

Growing up in my generation, everything was collectable - nothing was thrown away. So, like everyone else, I became a collector. Collections mean different things to many people. My first collection was during World War II. It was a collection of military men, trucks, and model airplanes. I started the collection at about age six and to this day, I do not know what ever happened to it as I grew up.

At age ten, I was on a pen-pal list with people abroad. I had pen-pals in Cuba, England, and Germany in my early teens. This was more of a hobby than a collection, even though I learned about foreign postage stamps, their currencies, and their cultures. One of my pen-pal relationships in England went on through the 1990s, until he passed away.

I guess I was a typical boy. My collections through childhood and into adulthood were beer cans, Coca-Cola, stamps, and currency of the world. Today, I have none of these collections because of moving around the country; most of my collection's items have disappeared from my household.

There are other collections that people save forever. This type of collection is called family heirlooms. Many people collect family heirlooms and pass them down through the generations. It is nice to say "this bed was my great-grandparents' from the 1880s," or "this set of China was my parents' wedding present," and "I can still drive my father's 1955 Chevy Bel Aire, even though it has over 200,000 miles on it."

In the late 20th and 21st centuries, our society has become a disposable society - when an item becomes less useful, it usually ends up in the landfill.

This is what a collector does when there are no family members interested in either collections or family heirlooms - they become giveaways to other people that can use them, or they go to charities like the Salvation Army, Habitat for Humanity, and even churches and rescue missions throughout the community. Though this donation process, we finally give away the memories we have valued through the years.

I believe that there will always be some people who will continue to collect items that are memories to them.

The Lady in the Floppy Pink Hat

This story was the result of an assignment designed by a group member's request that we write a story about each member of the group. I chose one of our group and decided to make it a humorous/moral of the story/mystery. I gave the group member a few props, and voila! She came to life.

-J. Vaughan

The Lady in the Floppy Pink Hat

She sat alone in the railcar seat, reading a fashion magazine, while tapping her foot in time to the rumble of the car over the tracks. I noticed her manicured nails, the well-coiffed hair, and the incongruent stain of red claw on her stately high heels.

I greeted her with, "Good Morning, Ma'am," and she barely acknowledged me with a slight nod that sent the floppy hat flopping vigorously. Her hand quickly slipped upward and swept the hat in one angry swat to the seat beside her. Glowering at me, she hissed and raised her magazine to resume her scan of the page in front of her.

A small child walked toward the floppy hat lady and began excitedly relating all of his adventures of the day. He picked up the voluminous pink mass beside her and installed himself as tightly close as a child can get to another person. I waited for what I assumed would be a violent act of revulsion, but to my complete astonishment, FPHL (as I shall call her heretofore) bent gently down, kissed the tot smack on his little head and carefully pulled him into her lap. Their conversation became an animated delight of wonderments found on the train, and happy hopes of what they could see at the journey's end. The lunch trays arrived, and FPHL busied herself by preparing his food, tucking the napkin squarely under his little chin, and singing a quaint little ditty about boys and trees and jumping puddles.

The conductor made his way through cars collecting tickets and punching them with a punch plier that was chained to his belt. When he reached the FPHL and the little boy, he asked for their tickets, and while punching them, surveyed them surreptitiously from top to bottom, then turned to me. I gave him my ticket, he looked at the date on it, then without handing it back, said, "Excuse me Sir, but I must ask you to come with me, please," and with that he grasped my coat and pulled me to my feet. In amazement, I followed him into the narrow hallway and was rapidly pulled toward another cabin, where he hoarsely told me to stay there until he came back for me. He then closed the door tightly behind him and I heard his steps hurriedly moving toward the next car.

A few moments later I heard shouting and banging about in the hallway. "Police!" Doors banged and I heard the FPHL protesting that she had not done anything wrong, followed by the high-pitched wail of the little boy who was being dragged alongside her.

I poked my head out of the doorway and was promptly shoved back inside by a burly copper who said, "Best mind your own, Gov'nor."

At the next stop all passengers were asked to depart the train, and we stood in a long queue on the platform while all of our belongings were searched. At length one of the officers yelled, "Found!" and rose with excitement having a pearl necklace dangling from his hand.

The bag from which the necklace was pulled, belonged to FPHL and they immediately hauled her off in handcuffs, and the head copper was pounding another man on the back, saying, "Well done! Well done!"

It turns out the FPHL was a notorious jewel thief and the little boy was her ruse to distract her marks while she pilfered their pockets.

The Moral of the Story:
Be careful with assumptions, because they will always lead you astray.

Reflection

This poem came about as I stared out the large sized porch window in the evening, seeing my body multiply through the window by bouncing off the window in the back wall.
        -Dawn Cunningham

Reflection

This window
-- in a room of many windows-- is
Unlike a mirror
But a mirror,
Nonetheless. It Reflects
An empty chair Indefinitely
In a corner,
Another mirror
Of mirrors of mirrors
Of my breast, my butt
But never
The waste,
Never
The heart.

How odd to think I can see Myself-- such a con.
A Transparency Of bones, Of muscles,
The continuance Of limbs
Trolling upon the world;
The imagined-me in the world,
Beyond my pane.

This Reflection:
The echo of music Without notes:
The trumpet that Beats out a base cord.
The scream Unscreened & The talk not Left to walk.
Doing the black & white,
While the troll within wants to get out.
Forgetting the evening Curtsy to the East
& the morning Bow to the West-- unconsciously, I ask.
The self I won't admit into My brain,
The self-fortress built by others.

The Reflection:
A lie-- I stare and I don't want to look.
Yet, it tells the seed within me it isn't
Who it believes to be.
The seed itself is unrecognizable
& controlled.

It Is Enough

- Denise K. Buhr

"It is a word we use every day, yet we are practically incapable of recognizing it when it's staring us in the face. The word is 'enough.'" - Joe Dominguez and Vicki Robin

It Is Enough

Not too little, not too much. Just enough. Enough food, enough clothes, enough stuff in a big enough house. Enough to do in a day that has enough value to be worth doing and enough time to play and pray and rest. And yet my life is too full. I have more than enough. So I strive to simplify. To unclutter. To buy only what I need when I need it. And more than that: to know what it is I *need* and not just what I *think* I want.

Yet I continuously fail. There's too much of "oh, that's cute," and "I want one of each," and "it's on sale so I really should stock up." I am brainwashed by the ads and the sales and want to be a good citizen so I succumb to our economy's need for me to be a consumer and I buy. Then I give away. Then buy some more and another trip to Goodwill.

But maybe there is redemption in my failure. If the shorts and shoes I give away will clothe someone who is naked, if the kitchen gadgets will help feed someone who was hungry, if the trinkets will comfort someone who is sick or in prison, maybe I will be on Jesus' "right hand" and welcomed into the kingdom.

But I would rather be more diligent about spending and give money where I *know* it will do good rather than *hoping* my cast-offs are of benefit. So I'll say a little prayer to resist temptation. I'll practice "stop before I shop" and ask myself if I really need IT.

Others don't always understand the deep longing I have for an unencumbered life. I use that word instead of simple, which has been so overused that it's been trivialized. When one talks about the simple life, many envision the Amish. I don't want the life of the "plain" people. They are being infected with the world's consumer ways like the rest of us. And I don't want a plain life. I want a life adorned with beauty and colored with love. Life isn't simple. It's complex and complicated. Maybe it's only our outlook that needs to be simple.

I hear my family and friends say the same thing as I do, "I have too much stuff," "I really need to clean out the closet . . . the garage . . . the basement . . . the whole house." We commiserate with one another, give each other advice neither of us listens to, and even occasionally hold each other accountable and help each other out. Perhaps I will never be as free from possessions as Jesus was, who depended on his friends and followers for his very food and shelter. But I can look forward identifying what's important in the rest of my life and letting the rest go. In the words of Christian singer Margaret Becker:

> *"I'm gonna give away the stereo*
> *Give away my TV*
> *I'm going back to essentials, a chair and a lamp*
> *And the Book that You wrote for me*
> *You see, I'm looking for the You that used to speak*
> *to clear*
> *I'm looking for the me that had a heart to hear."*

Hug

I wrote this poem two days after I had my first memory-induced PTSD attack that I have had in years. It was during an IPFW Ladder UPP™ Creative Writing Group meeting. It caught me completely by surprise, and I was so rattled by it that the other members noticed. Knowing how I felt, Dawn got up and gave me a hug, silently holding me for as long as I needed it.

That hug spoke more to me in that moment than any number of words could.
-ML Wissing

Hug

Arms wrapped around me
In the middle of the fight,
Carrying me from the monsters and
Closer to the light.
Tears fall upon the shoulder
Pressed against my cheek,
Strength in torso and heart
To all upon when I feel weak.
Companionship and love
Hold the sneaking shadows at bay,
The still air is quiet,
No words we need to say.
In the grasp of the memories
A silent cry for help,
The comfort of a hug reminds me
I am not by myself.

Tinnitus

Tinnitus, or ringing in the ears, have been a major function of my life. I first thought it was due to the time I spent in the military. My duties included listening to Morse Code through headsets. I had related the Tinnitus to this activity but it may not be where it first began.
-John D. Hannigan

Tinnitus

A few years ago, I applied through the Veteran's Administration for a hearing disability for the Tinnitus. I probably should have applied back when I got out of military service. The VA awarded me a service-connected disability and provided me with a set of hearing aids. They are designed to affect only high frequencies. Actually, they have not helped with the continual ringing in my ears. It has gotten worse as I have grown older.

I was advised that the Tinnitus is incurable until recently. My Tinnitus is more in my left ear than my right and unless you have Tinnitus, you have no idea how irritating it is on a daily basis.

In a discussion with my wife, we reviewed why I would have had Tinnitus most of my life and why it got worse as I grew older. Incidentally, that is what my Veterans' Affairs hearing tests indicated in addition to high frequency loss.

I had mastoid problems with my ears when I was a young child. I had earaches during my years growing up in school, however I did not have the continual ringing in my ears. I did have times when my ears felt like they were full of water or something that caused me to loss of hearing. During the discussion, it was determined that my ringing in the ears might have come because of a trauma as a child. I have never had a ruptured eardrum, so it might be caused by a nerve. Other than what I mentioned earlier of mastoid problems, what could the trauma be?

I recalled as a child and even through my teenage years that my mother, when angry at me, she would slap me across the left side of the face as punishment. This is of course something that she had encountered in her growing up as a child. If it worked for Grandpa and grandma then that was the punishment she elected to use to discipline me. Evidently the face slapping had done some damage over the years and the ringing in my ears became louder and louder as I grew up. In addition, my military service aggravated the condition.

After all these years, I now know the original cause of my Tinnitus. However, as I mentioned earlier, I still have ringing in the ears.

JML and the JD

My most vivid memory of a goal set decades ago, began in a one-room country school room. Sitting in a wooden desk whose lid lifted up and had a special well for an ink bottle, I remember seeing pictures of students in a university listening to a professor lecture. I decided that I wanted to be one of those professors and earn the right to wear the hooded robes of a terminal degree. I am on my way to that goal, only one more degree to go before I die.

- J. Vaughan

JML and the JD

Hey Dad!

Sorry it's been so long since I wrote to you. I always say I'm really busy, but that is never a good excuse. I'll try to stay in touch more often.

Did I tell you that I finally got my long hair cut off? Yeah, I had a heart to heart with my mirror and I knew it was time. All that beautiful red/auburn hair has turned to a mix of white/grey/blonde and having it so very long was really making me look haggard to say the least! I have a great stylist and she was extra patient with me as she began to cut and style the hair, all while I was trying hard not to cry while giving in to a few heavy sighs. I used to make fun of blondes, saying that while blondes were supposedly "having more fun" the redheads were actually out there enjoying life to the full. Karma sucks sometimes, you know?! I'll post a few pics on FB in case you are checking in on my newsfeed.

Thanks for the super blessing in the mail. I needed to pay some bills and you were right on time, as always. How did you know? Are you stalking me? Hah! Those independently wealthy folks have nothing on me-my Dad really knows how to bless a child! All those years of living below the poverty level, working three jobs, always wondering why my hard work wasn't translating into wealth; I guess my mindset still has me believing that I don't deserve or can't afford the best in life. I *know* in my heart that I am worthy, but the concrete proving of it keeps stopping me from living my worth in the reality of now.

I actually finished my law degree in three years, how about that! Yes, the ceremony is going to be held on Friday evening; so happy that you are going to be able to be there. Getting my "hood" is something that I've wanted all of my life, and that is one dream that you helped me to keep alive through all the messes I've made of my life. Thank you for your encouragement, love, and steadfastly reminding me that I am your daughter and nothing is too good for me, or beyond my reach. Wow! "Juris Doctorate"! No one ever thought that the little red-haired girl from Riverdale who wasn't even tall enough to reach the pencil sharpener, would someday stand on a college stage to receive a doctoral degree. The best they could conceive of for me was to get married and have children. Been there did that, lost the t-shirt! Can't believe that my babies now have babies, and Nana finally made "JD".

This dream finally came true. I often wondered why it wouldn't just die, but it never did... It was like this small light inside of me that kept showing up on my darkest days. Friday evening, I will dedicate this degree to you and hope that in some small way I have made you proud.

I'm looking forward to the drive next week. All my "stuff" has been either sold or given away – best purge ever! The few things I kept are already packed in the truck ready for my new adventure. Great truck Dad! Nothing "compact" about it! Four wheel drive, fold down seats, rack on top, metallic cherry red, black leather interior, and a CD player that kicks some big butt! I really don't need all that space, but that doesn't mean I won't enjoy having it! There is nothing like hitting the highway for a new adventure in the vehicle of your dreams.

Do you remember how tiny my Shetland Sheep puppy was in December? Well, I'm glad that the Captain's bucket seat in the truck is big. That organic puppy chow you told me about has made Bella grow pretty fast, good thing she isn't a large breed dog!

The Bella girl and I are so ready to smell the salt air. Man, it's going to be so great to sink my toes into the sand, hear my buddies the sea lions barking, and feel the ocean wind blasting my hair in every direction. The first run on the beach is going to be glorious, yeah! Should I have a bonfire on the beach that first night? I checked the weather and the wind is supposed to calm down around seven or so. The truck has room for some chairs and I can get firewood at the little store by the beach.

Oh, I forgot to tell you, the house is perfect! Thank you so much for all of your hard work. Those driftwood pieces are so cool, and you did a wonderful job with the paint colors. Soft white and ocean blue, with hemp rugs and wall hangings – I'll think I am heaven every time I wake up! Thanks for the special bed for Bella-the trick will be getting her to sleep there instead of on my bed. She has been such a blessing in my life, so I really shouldn't complain, but she does snore you know! LOL!

The kitchen is awesome with that quarry tile counter, space for the herb plants on the window sill over the sink, French door fridge, and counter range top. I laughed the first time I saw the baking island with the sink-was that a hint for some sweet rolls? Blue and white striped curtains on the French doors to the patio, made it feel airy and light. The ocean breeze will be able to send the scent of rhubarb pie baking all over the beach. I think my kitchen will be a "must stop" place for the locals on baking days!

The antique desk on the sun porch is going to get some serious use over the next year. The last book in the series still needs a few chapters, and I think that is going to be the absolutely most inspiring place to work. I wonder how many authors have used fountain pens to scrawl their manuscripts; thanks for the graduation gift, and no I won't tell how much it cost for just ONE pen! You are such a character, Dad!

Bella and I are going to leave before first light on Saturday, so we should arrive at the beach by dinner time. I am thinking soft shell crab chowder and chocolate raspberry cheesecake to celebrate. I will stop at the crab shack on the way into the village and pick up a crock of chowder and the bakery is just down the block from the cottage. I guess that is all for now.

Love always,
JML

Not Her Daddy

This tidbit came about after seeing photos of my granddaughter holding her first fish, which was posted on FaceBook by her mother.
- Dawn Cunningham

Not Her Daddy

I had a hard time deciding where I wanted to put this entry: personal journal or one of my blog sites. I chose a blog site—probably two, by the time it has been placed on the internet. Anyhow, this deals with emotions stemming from seeing my granddaughter being taught how to fish by another man. It isn't about begrudging her the opportunity or being mad at this man who isn't her daddy; this is about the "it isn't fair" emotion because cancer decided to take Vincent away. When I first saw the picture, I thought, Wow! She caught a fish! Then, realizing it wasn't her daddy there doing it with her, my smile and enthusiasm diminished. It should be her daddy doing this with her. Then I thought, her uncle should be doing it with her. I am happy she caught a fish. I am happy she experienced this. I am happy someone is there to teach her (hopefully ethically). I've only met her stepfather once. I can't say much about him. I only know what trickles down to me from others, and I must be careful in making a decision in what type of man he is. As a parent, I understand how a parent is critical about the chosen partner of a child. It continues on for a lifetime. That's being a parent—protective. As I said, I don't know her stepfather. I can only tell you what I felt as I saw the photograph. It's hard! It's terribly hard!

I know how much Vincent loved fishing. I remember him saying he was going to teach Chloe how to fish and to hunt—especially fish. His attitude was about having a girl that could be prissy and boyish. How much he would have accomplished depended on Sammie too (smirking as I think about it). Yes, I began to see Vincent in that photograph with Chloe sitting on his knee as the fish dangled from the fishing pole. That's where Vincent should have been.

If anyone thinks this emotion is wrong, YOU ARE WRONG. An emotion is exactly what it needs to be because God gave them to us—all of them! It's what you do with an emotion that decides right or wrong. So, I took the time to cry and took the time to discuss it with Chris. No matter, I will always have this feeling and need to deal with it—someone other raising my boy's little girl. I can't change what happened to Vincent; I can't change how I feel; the only control I have is to face it and deal with it. AND PLEASE don't tell me I can change how I feel—if you haven't been in my position, you have no place telling me a thing. I'm sure other grandparents out there understand.

You Are Loved

The holidays are a hard time of year. With the guilt of my mother's death on my mind, it still hurts more than ever. It took a long while before I could really feel anything during the holiday season, especially Christmas.

-ML Wissing

You Are Loved

I dressed up as Santa
To sit in the mall,
Just for the money
Not feeling Christmassy at all.

I just needed the money
To keep on my lights,
I silently groaned
As I looked at the lines.

Kids all sat and told me
Of what they wanted this year,
But to be honest,
I really didn't hear.

"Ho, ho, ho," I mustered,
With a lot of fake cheer,
Tired of kids whining,
Their tugging my beard.

Hours went on
Would this never end?
I swear I would scream
If I had to do this again.

A small little girl
Was up next in line,
Great now what,
Would it be a pony this time?

She climbed into the sleigh
And onto my thigh,
She gestured to come closer,
I leaned in and grumpily sighed.

The girl leaned up
And whispered in my ear
"Well, Santa," she said,
"My mommy died this year."

"It wasn't my fault
But I still feel the blame,
And Christmas without Mommy
Just doesn't feel the same.

Mommy and I argued,
When we should have hugged,
Could you tell her, Santa,
Can you tell her she was loved?

Please tell her I'm sorry
And I miss her so much,
I just want this for Christmas;
I don't want presents and such.

That's all I have
On my Christmas list,
I'll do anything you ask, Santa,
If you could do this."

I slowly nodded,
Nothing in my head sounded right,
I couldn't even speak,
My throat grew too tight.

She got off my lap
And out of the wooden sleigh,
Another kid came over
But I couldn't look away.

I finally looked down,
A tear in my eye.
It wouldn't do the kids good
To see ol' Santa cry.

Later I went to my car
And I sat down and cried.
I felt something stirring
In the heart that once had died.

I had started believing
In this world full of sin
That the Spirit of Christmas died,
And would never live again.

I looked at the stars,
Bowed my head to pray.
I hadn't done this in years,
What would I say?

"Dear Lord," I said,
"This Christmas Eve night,
Please watch over the girl,
Guide her with Your light."

I felt more than heard
A Voice in my ear,
It wasn't quite hearing it,
But there was no doubt it was there.

"The greatest Christmas gift
Doesn't come under a tree,
It isn't something
That's for the world to see.

The greatest Christmas gift
Is from the Heavens above,
The greatest words ever known:
"You are loved."

I have suffered with PTSD for years. I had an opportunity to attend a Ladder UPP™ course in order to learn how to accept my flashbacks and dreams and to write a short story about each event. These are some of my writings. I still have PTSD but Ladder UPP™ gave me the opportunity to deal with it.
*   - John D. Hannigan*

No Stopping, No Standing, No Parking, No U-Turn: One Way

- Denise K. Buhr

"When you were born, you cried and the world rejoiced. Live your life in such a manner that when you die the world cries and you rejoice." -Proverb

"I really and truly believe in God with all kinds of doubts." -Madeleine L'Engle

No Stopping, No Standing, No Parking, No U-Turn: One Way

[As the lights come up, Mags is sitting on the "ground" outside a tall wall with a narrow gate in it. Peter is on the inside of the wall, looking out over the top at her.]

PETER: How long are you going to sit there?

MAGS: As long as it takes. Forever if I have to.

PETER: Forever is a long time.

MAGS: I have all the time there is, don't I? That's what eternity is, right?

PETER: It's a lot nicer inside than it is out there. You could be enjoying your time instead of... well, not. It's a great place.

MAGS: I know. Inside that pearly gate are streets paved with gold and a mansion for everyone. By the way, who cleans those mansions? Do we each get a staff of angels who take care of the place and brings us our heavenly manna? Now there's one things I regret-- I never had a cleaning service when I was alive.

PETER: Heaven does not need to be cleaned.

MAGS: That's right; it's perfect.

PETER: And I will remind you that you *are* alive right now.

MAGS: Yeah. And I'm having a great time. I've got a comfy seat on this cloud, watching the world go by. I got a nice white robe with lots of room to breathe, a pair of wings to cool me off if I get too hot. Of course, this being heaven I probably won't need them as much as I would in the other place. And I have this lovely harp to entertain us. You won't mind if I hit a few sour notes, will you? I was never musically inclined.

PETER: Those old clichés aren't funny. And they're not true. Heaven's not like that.

MAGS: But I'm not in heaven yet. And I do have you to talk to.

PETER: What if I leave?

MAGS: You're the gatekeeper. You can't leave. You have to be here to let new souls in whenever they arrive. I have arrived.

PETER: And I'm waiting to let you in.

MAGS: I am on the list, aren't I?

PETER: Of course. Or you wouldn't be out there. You'd be... outside the other place.

MAGS: Can I see the list?

PETER: I can't show you the list.

MAGS: Why not? I want to see if my friend is on the list. She should be. Really. And she should be along any time now. She wasn't doing too well the last time I saw her. She has cancer. But you probably already know that. And you probably also know that I had just been to the hospital to see her when that stupid bus lost control on the ice and... well, here I am. She promised she'd wait for me cause we thought she'd get here first so I'm gonna do the same for her. At least tell me if she's on the list. Her name is Liz.

[Peter pulls up a laptop or tablet and starts typing.]

MAGS: Really? A computer document? What happened to the long parchment scrolls?

PETER: Passé. We do keep up with the times here. And it's actually a spreadsheet.

MAGS: What do you need besides a name?

PETER: There are a lot of John Smiths, you know. We need home address, various contact information...

MAGS: God sends emails?

PETER: He could, of course. But He prefers the usual. Rainbow dreams, burning bushes, stubborn asses.

MAGS: Say what?

PETER: Balaam's donkey. Numbers 22. Look it up. Where was I? Date of the first faith declaration, prayer requests, sheep and goat acts...

MAGS: Goat acts? That sounds rude.

PETER: Acts of kindness. Or not. "If you did for the least of these, you did it for me."

MAGS: Oh. The story of Judgement Day. The sheep on the right, the goats on the left. What is with the idea that the bad guys have to be on the left and the good guys on the right? Don't lefties have a hard enough time as it is? If I remember right... correctly... the sheep fed hungry people and gave them water and visited them when they were sick. So I got a check mark every time I visited Liz? Cool. What else is on that spreadsheet?

PETER: It doesn't matter. Either your name is here or it's not.

MAGS: So all those people down there... it is down, isn't it? Earth, I mean. Are we really *up*? I guess we are if I can see that blue little marble below me, just like the guys on the Apollo moon missions. I was never very good with directions. Anyway, you know some people on earth think heaven as this exclusive place, a kind of country club where only people just like them can get in. Obviously it's not exclusive if I can get in, 'cause I'm certainly that kind of person. I don't have the "right stuff." Well, I guess I do really because of John 3:16. You know what that is?

PETER: I'm familiar with it.

MAGS: So what about the others?

PETER: The others?

MAGS: The ones who dig wells for people in poor countries so they can have clean water. The ones who go to places where there are epidemics of deadly diseases and take care of the sick. The ones who feed the hungry and put clothes on the naked. And *aren't* Christians?

PETER: You know what the Bible says. The only way into heaven is to believe in Jesus Christ.

MAGS: And I know what supposedly happens to the Muslims and the Buddhists and the Hindus and the atheists and the agnostics and even the Jews. Like Jesus said to the goats, "Depart from me, ye cursed, into everlasting fire, prepared for the devil and his angels."

PETER: So?

MAGS: So, here's the problem. My friend Liz. We never really talked about faith and what she believed and all that. I mean, from what she's said, I think she believes in God, or a god, but she's not a church-goer. But she's the sweetest, kindest, gentlest, most loving, generous, and giving person I've ever met. She'd do anything for anyone whether they deserved it or not. Your spreadsheet isn't big enough for all the "sheep" checkmarks she'd have. And there'd be a big fat zero on the "goat" side. And yet...

PETER: And yet?

MAGS: And yet, Liz very well could have one *helluva* forever even though Jesus said the sheep get to go to heaven because of their good deeds.

PETER: You don't get to heaven because of what you do. You get to heaven because of what you believe. What you do is a reflection of that belief.

MAGS: So a murderer gets a free pass because he's a "believer" and says he's sorry, and Liz gets wailing and gnashing of teeth. Well, that's just screwed up.

PETER: First of all, it's not for you to judge. Secondly, God doesn't make mistakes.

MAGS: Okay, call it a contradiction. God is love, right? I mean that's the nature of God. It's the elemental essence of God's very being. That's what it says in the first letter of John, chapter four, verse sixteen. See, I can cite book, chapter *and* verse. "God is love. Whoever lives in love lives in God, and God in him." Or if you want to stick to the classic King James... you know that man had a way with words. Well, his flunkies did. Anyway, back to the verse. "He that loveth not knoweth not God; for God is love." If God is love, how can He condemn any human being? The pinnacle of creation, formed by God's own hands and not just spoken into existence. Created in God's own image, for Pete's sake! Oops. Sorry. It's just an expression.

PETER: No offense taken. I've heard it before. A thousand times ten thousand and more.

MAGS: Kind of like forgiveness. Not seven times but seventy times seven? You remember that?

PETER: Yes.

MAGS: So back to my original question. How can God condemn even one person to hell? Fire and brimstone, the bottomless pit, darkness forever? That's just awful.

PETER: From your Bible reading you know that God is also righteous.

MAGS: Yeah. God is righteous. God has rules. I'm just asking; doesn't God have a backup plan? Can't people go to another planet and try it again? Reincarnated on another world? I mean there's a lot of universe out there.

PETER: That's what you think God should do? Give everyone down there - and yes, up here we say down there - give everyone a second chance? Once wasn't enough?

MAGS: No. How about seventy times seven more chances? Those seem to be popular numbers with God. Besides, what's a few more million years compared to forever? It makes more sense than saying, "I'm everlasting love and I love everyone (but hate their sins, of course), but, so sorry, you blew it. You had your chance. Now go away and have a miserable existence for the rest of your eternal life. Forever?" How can God live with himself? That'd be tearing me up inside.

PETER: How do you know it's not doing the same to God?

MAGS: If it is, He ought to fix it! That's basically saying He's God but He's powerless to save them. If that's true, then how can He be God?!

PETER: "'For my thoughts are not your thoughts, neither are your ways my ways,' declares the Lord." Isaiah, the 55th chapter, verse 8.

MAGS: You're pretty good at quoting the Old Testament.

PETER: That's all there was when I was down there. The other part - we were living it, not reading it. And I can't answer your questions. I'm just like you.

MAGS: No you're not. You're the Rock. Not like "the Rock," the wrestler.

PETER: But I did wrestle with my faith. I'm human and had doubts and fears and didn't always understand. You know that. My life was an open book.

MAGS: Four books, actually.

PETER: Five, but who's counting. None of the boys showed me in a very good light. Unfortunately what they wrote were the facts. Even at the end, when I tried to be the Rock, I didn't know everything. But I believed. I believed in Him and His word. And I believed that one day I would learn the truth, all the truth, on the day that I saw Him again.

MAGS: And did you?

PETER: Yes. And no. Remember, this is God we're talking about. If we live forever - and we will - we'll never have all of our questions answered. There are too many. But once you step through this gate, you'll find that you don't have any questions at all. It's heaven.

MAGS: Literally? Or figuratively?

PETER: Come in and you'll see.

MAGS: God can't change His mind about me, can He?

PETER: What do you mean?

MAGS: From what I know and what we've been talking about, I've got heaven locked up, so to speak. I mean, I'm dead. I can't change what I believe anymore so I'm going to get in whenever I decide to go in. I haven't given up my "backstage" pass or my ticket to paradise.

PETER: The gate is forever open to you to come in.

MAGS: I think I'll sit out here a little longer then.

PETER: But you're creating delays in the process.

MAGS: What do you mean?

PETER: You're not the only one who died today.

MAGS: You mean there are a few more who get to knock and have the door opened for them?

PETER: There is a lot more. And you're holding up the queue.

MAGS: The Q? Oh. I don't see a queue. Just a wiggly line of sparkly things. Oh! Are those...

PETER: The other souls that passed into eternity today.

MAGS: In other words, they got their tickets punched! Hey, come on up!

PETER: They can't. I have to take them in in the same order that they died.

MAGS: That could take... forever! Get it? I am on a roll today!

PETER: As I once said, "With the Lord a day is like a thousand years, and a thousand years are like day."

MAGS: You said that? Really? Who knew you could learn something new even after you were dead. What if two people died at the exact same time, like a car accident? Who gets to go in first? 'Cause that gate is not very wide.

PETER: There is no such thing as the exact same time. God knows time in infinitely smaller measures than your hours, minutes, or seconds. Everyone is born and dies at their own unique time.

MAGS: So no one else can enter heaven until I do? It seems we're stuck between a rock and a hard place. Maybe you want to send out a legion of angels with some b'manna bread. For another miraculous feeding. Or they could flame-broil some mannaburgers for those a little closer to you-know-where.

PETER: You know, if your friend Liz is in this line, she can't get any closer until you go in.

MAGS: Then tell me! Tell me if she's on the list.

PETER: I can't. It's not for you to know, while you're out there.

MAGS: Then I can't go in.

PETER: Why not?

MAGS: If I go in and the gate closes behind me, I can't ever leave again.

PETER: True. But why would you want to?

MAGS: If Liz isn't on that stupid computer of yours, I'll never see her again. I can't live with that, not for eternity.

PETER: You won't feel like that once you're in heaven. Your joy here is perfect.

MAGS: If I'm happy and she's not here that means I forgot about her. That's not perfection. That's amnesia. I don't want to forget Liz. Ever.

PETER: You can't help her now anyway so…

MAGS: Don't say it.

PETER: There's nothing more to say. And only one thing you can do.

[Peter and his computer disappear behind a wall and the gate slowly opens. Mags stands in front of it as the lights fade, leaving only the opening of the gate lit, until that too goes dark.]

Cold Arms

I sat outside wondering what it looked like watching me live in the shadow of a man who saw me as a child. This is what came of that imagination.
- Dawn Cunningham

Cold Arms

It is Friday. The children play in the April's cold rain with winter coats on. He has left for work. I can see her standing in the shadows, looking out the screen door window, watching the children. I can see tears hidden behind her eyes, which shades the day more than rain. Her movement, or lack of movement, to lean her shoulder onto the framework to enjoy, to relax, just for bit. . . . I can smell chicken soup escape from the house. One boy rakes stones in the drive, filling in the pit that sinks daily. A blue jay chats with a cardinal above him - probably a discussion about the boy and the weather - as the rain trickles between the branches. The girl's pink bike lays on the sidewalk that leads to the garage, staring at the previous owners' old crumpled rabbit cage, which still holds fur from when the little girl tried to rescue Blacky from a snake. Interstate 69 roars uncontrollably. Rain doesn't drain the sound into the ground.

Harder rain, harder eyes, cold heart, stones scrambled, fur balled, walls are drain pipes. Memories compiled in a box. When will she leave? I know when. . . I just know: before it's too late   for me.

Adolescence

I learned in college that getting your problems out on paper, in song, or even speaking them aloud is called "externalizing", and by helping you get the feelings, frustration, and guilt out from inside you, relieving stress off the mind and body. It is an important part of therapy and can begin helping the person find solutions, or just to feel better in general.

Even though it went through a few drafts, this piece was a hard one for me to write and even harder for me to read afterward. It brought back memories I had thought long buried, yet at the same time, writing them out helped me face them. It continued the healing process, and began strengthening me at the same time; much like how a broken bone heals stronger.

I decided to include this piece as a way to show that even though a person has gone through so much, there is so much more inside of them that is positive, and it takes determination and strength to fight through it and find a way out of the darkness.

It certainly is true that you never know how strong you are until being strong is all you have left.
- ML Wissing

Adolescence

In school, as in life, she was taught there are three major stages of life: childhood, adolescence, and adulthood - that it was the way all of humanity goes through life, in a set pattern. So, she sat in sociology class, pondering what in the world went wrong with her. She was thrust from childhood to adulthood almost immediately, with nothing in between. There were no stages for the self-discovery that came with the stage more commonly known as adolescence.

When she was born in another country, she was supposed to have died. Only by a miracle did she survive. She later found a diary of her mother, stating that she had wanted to kill her when she saw her for the first time. It was unclear to her young mind that her mother only wished to spare her a life of pain and misery of complications she may have.

She had met her childhood with told stories of repeated rapes echoing in her ears, a fear of men soon commanding her heart and mind. At ten, she swore never to have sex until marriage, spurred by the fears of men and being raped. She stood up to bullies who targeted her deaf sister. Her first date came and went at thirteen, and her boyfriend told her to stay away from male friends, and she stood up to him. She never kissed him. But he'd wait for her to come outside to be with him, watching her through the windows of her home as she did chores, something her mother knew and never told her until years later when it no longer mattered.

Two years later, she was molested by someone she counted as a family member, he fifty-eight years old. When she told her friends, they made her tell a teacher, who told her parents. But when the school found out, they shunned her and her family. Word got out around town, and they too turned their backs on them, for half of the town were related, and were friends with the popular granddaughter of the male who had touched her wrongly. Suddenly she was alone, carrying a teddy bear to class in her backpack as her only friend and companion. Her father's company moved them across the state to get away from it, but it was too late, depression had set in.

Years went, she never laughing, never smiling. She only spoke when she had to. She hid her body behind clothing too large for her, she hid her face behind a curtain of hair. The one boyfriend she did have for six months dumped her when he found out she had been molested years before.

She moved across the country with her family and started to open up again in her new school, making a few close friends. She began to have a boyfriend, the most popular male in the grade below her asking her out. Junior prom came, and a night that started so wonderfully ended abruptly when he pulled her out of the gym and into the hallway and dumped her, before walking back inside to enjoy the rest of prom without her. It did nothing but crush her once again.

Years of abuse, trauma, and humiliation worked in her heart and mind. Every time she tried to better herself, she was knocked down. She joined the military, and after announcing it, family and friends asked her parents, "isn't she too weak?" It hurt, hearing how many people didn't believe in her, but she went anyway, partially a way to get away and attempt to find herself.

She found herself in the arms of a male who pushed and pushed until she gave up her virginity. He made her regret it every day, taking her to bed, even if she was physically ill or not feeling like it. For years this went on, she was finding out he had been stalking her through the relationship as well. She gained the courage to leave him, and found herself still being stalked.

He worked in a similar section of the military, so they would run into each other sometimes. He once sang a cadence about her in front of over 100 people, they sang along with it, not realizing the story behind it or who it was about. He grabbed her once as she walked away, and martial art instinct kicked in, she almost breaking his elbow, but didn't, because she didn't want him pressing charges against her and making things worse for her.

She went to Iraq, taken from her friends, and again had to find herself. Her stalker ex began calling her at work there, for he was in country, but further away. He sent her an insulting letter via Certified Mail, humiliating her further, driving down her self-worth. She kept the letter, over a decade later, to remind herself that people are not always what they seem to be.

She was raped while in Iraq, and her unit blamed her. She was met with looks, whispers, rumors about her. Even the people who were investigating the incident, who had said the man had confessed to them everything, said they thought she was lying to her face. Her friends she met out in country were ordered to stay away from her. Once again, she was alone. When it was time to leave the country, she wanted to stay in Iraq or Kuwait, not wanting to return to the United States because she feared her ex finding her again.

She finally grew to care for further a friend who was in Iraq with her who was told to stay from her, but remained at her side as a support. She moved in with him, and got engaged. Three years later, he was given two weeks' notice to deploy to Iraq. She and he got married in a hospital chapel during a blizzard, and a day later he was shipped off. While he was gone not even two months, she received word her mother had completed suicide. Two months after that, her boss pulled her aside and asked her to leave the company. She'd worked there for almost ten years, and was a manager-in-training, on the way to obtain her own store. Now, once again, she was all alone.

She was depressed deeply, given antidepressants to keep her stable. For years she felt a complete failure, not letting more than a few get closer to her, not leaving the house. She began drinking daily.

But slowly, she began to discover herself. She stopped drinking, obtained a driver's' license, something she never did due to fearing being alone and someone attacking her. She started college classes at a nearby campus. She began to experience life, experimenting with her hair, nails, looks, clothing.

She had gone through adulthood and reached a late adolescence, skipping the steps in the pattern to create her own. Her husband says she sometimes acts like she is younger than she is, that he feels he is taking care of a child, or a teenager.

Perhaps in a way he is, because she is testing her boundaries, testing herself, and finding she has her own wings to fly.

Amish Trip, October 2009

Karen [my wife] and I had the opportunity to visit with both Amish and Mennonite families during the month of October in 2009. The experience of living with two different Amish families, then a Mennonite family, differed from our culture and living style.
-John D. Hannigan

Amish Trip, October 2009

During our first stop in the Amish community of Interlaken, New York, we stayed with the Fischer family for one night and the next day. Driving down the streets was an experience; there were no lights, just pitch black driving. We arrived at the Fischer family about 10:30 p.m. and were greeted by Sarah, the mother, with a lantern. We learned that the father and children were already in bed for the night. She told us that they had nine children; six boys and three girls.

The Amish have no radio, television, or electricity. The father and mother have no wedding rings, since it is against their culture to wear jewelry. Their women do not wear makeup. It is a simple lifestyle, strictly by the Amish culture. They use only battery lanterns and kerosene lights after dark to light their way.

The Amish home is two stories. There is a large room on the bottom floor that consists of the kitchen, dining area, and a relaxation area. There are two adjacent rooms that are used for the children's play area and gatherings of community people. The house was cold except for the coal stove on the lower floor, and there is no central air or heat, only the stove. The master bedroom is also on the first floor. There is a bathroom on the first floor as well. Their children sleep upstairs, which usually has four bedrooms with a bathroom upstairs. She took us upstairs to a bedroom for the night.

Early the next morning, we got up and went downstairs for breakfast. We noticed that there was a wooden family tree listing their genealogy. All of the children were up and seated at the table according to their age, oldest to youngest. The father sat at the head of the table and the mother sat next to him on his left. I sat at the other end of the table and Karen sat to my right. We all ate with our spoons and left our dishes clean; usually there are no leftovers at the end of a meal. The Amish food is rich, with most of it made from scratch.

It appeared that the father was the man of the house and his wife and children were subservient to him. When he spoke, no one else talked, but listened. The father and mother spoke in their language, so it was hard to understand what or whom they were talking about. They also spoke English. The father was rather a harsh person, the mother was very quiet and spoke in a low voice.

The father and the other men, as well as his oldest son, worked all day in the fields bringing corn stocks to the silo for winter storage. They used horses and wagons to bring the stocks in from the field. The silos had a gas-driven motor that pushed the corn stocks into it. The mother made a lunch for them at noon, and they went back to their chores with the corn stocks and silo.

We learned that the Amish children usually have a second-grade education and then they work around the home. The boys help their father while the girls help their mother. Five of the Fischer children went to school and the four youngest were at home playing and helping their mother.

Their language is Pennsylvania Dutch, a dialect of Low German. The children learn to understand and speak Pennsylvania Dutch at a young age. When the parents speak, the children listen; only one voice is heard. Some of the children never master the English language, however both the parents and some of the children are bilingual.

The transportation is horse and a wagon that is partially enclosed to protect the riders from the wind. The wagons have a reflective red triangle on the back indicating a slow vehicle. They have no State Driver's License, as pictures are not accepted by the Amish according to their culture.

What surprised me was the fact that the family had the capability of electricity in their home through the use of a portable generator with different out-power to support both A/C and D/C currents.

We left Interlaken with a better appreciation of the Amish ways. The next stop was Newburg, Pennsylvania. When we arrived it was early morning. This was the home of an elderly couple. We met the husband and a group of people, some Amish, some not. Their living conditions were similar to the Fischer family in Interlaken. They heated their home with propane gas and yet it was very cold. They had their families' children's, and grandchildren's, genealogy posted on a wall, as well as the husband's genealogy posted on the wall next to it.

These people were business people as well as farmers. The husband built utility sheds and gazebos for sale to people. The wife spent some of her daily time sewing, quilting, and selling her products. Their schedule was quite different than that of the Fischer family. Most of the Amish are in a business besides farming. The boys take up their father's trade at an early age while the girls learn their mother's trades. When a boy reaches about sixteen years of age, he is usually well-trained in his father's trade and then apply for certified licenses in the trades; carpentry, electricity, roofing, masoning, just to name a few. They usually start a business of their own or follow in their father's business.

They grow their own vegetables, fruit, meat, and dairy products. They buy what they cannot grow or sew. A good source for buying what they cannot do on their own is the Walmart store.

We slept upstairs that night in a cold bedroom. Early the next morning we came downstairs. We left around six in the morning to go to the lady's sister in Lancaster for the day. On the way, we stopped and had breakfast in a restaurant. When we arrived, we were well received and welcomed into the home. The living conditions were about the same as the previous Amish homes that we had stayed in.

That evening we left for a return trip to Newburg, and spent the night once again. Early the next morning we got up and went downstairs to see the lady had a breakfast of eggs, toast, ground sausage already started for us. After we ate we said our goodbyes and left for a Mennonite home in Hagerstown, Maryland.

Arriving in Hagerstown, I was amazed to see the difference in living conditions. This family was also elderly, but they lived in a modern home within city limits with all the comforts of our own home in Fort Wayne, Indiana. They had electricity, telephone, radio, and family pictures. Mennonites have vehicles and both the husband and the wife drive. The family we visited owned a grocery store and were of the Brethren Church.

One thing I did notice was there were no bottled gas or large propane tanks on their property, unlike the Amish.

The visit was nice and friendly, we having discussions about health issues, religion, and current news issues. We had a light lunch that afternoon, and left in the early evening to go out to dinner with our hosts. After dinner, we found a motel for the night before journeying back home once again.

I Wish

This was our first collaboration piece. Mary Arnold-Schwartz brought in several objects. Each participant chose one and wrote about ourselves based on that particular item. We then paired up, read each other's pieces, and chose phrases or lines from the other persons' work that we found interesting, intriguing, insightful-- something that caught our attention. We wrote these on cards, laid them out on the table, and as a group, decided which ones to use and in what order to arrange them.

Afterward, we took scissors and cut out important lines, then laid them on a table and created a poem from them. We all thought it came out pretty cool. Although some of our members have come and gone, we wanted this to be included in the book.

Members involved with this project:
Julie Dominguez
Julie Creek
J. Vaughan
Denise K Buhr
ML Wissing
Stevens Amidon
Mary Arnold-Schwartz
Mike Riff

I Wish

I always showed up for lunch
Plates, pretty pieces of glass
Whole inside
It's not meant to be perfect
It's still appreciated

Fear
Fights back tears
Maybe we'll just remember
I've also spent a lot of time being blue
White cotton blouses

Piles of little clothes, blankets, and toys
I saved his first pair of shoes
His mangled stuffed gorilla whose nose had been
chewed off
Tiny T-shirts and socks
His Winnie-the-Pooh baseball jacket

I didn't bother my brother
Stepdad puffs his chest
Tap. Tap. Tap.
Began to paint myself
It was what I was taught

Cerulean sky filled with fluffy clouds
Back to the city park for more sports
I don't think he ever saw me play
Whip of his arm
Bat connects with the ball

Come on, Jimmi, girl!
You got this!!

Pride oozing from every pore
See it fly, no, sail!
New girl in Catholic School
Painted smile, my momma-face,
Can be tough and pretty

It kept me occupied
Skittish around women with strong personalities

Purpose

Trying to make sense of the future while my "here and now" is so complex and fluid, led to this work on trying to decide what I would most enjoy doing before I die. This type of free flow thinking has led me to make great strides in forward momentum and fun risk taking that opened doors heretofore unimagined.

- J. Vaughan

Purpose

When I first wake up in the morning each day, my purpose is determined by... several different factors, some of which include the most-remembered species of that night's dream sequences or by the temperature in the room, or what racing thoughts are keeping me from focusing on the "normal" routines of the day.

I would like to believe that there is a rhyme and reason to my purpose that conveniently changes from day to day-- a real focus on my core values and beliefs, but the actuality is that stress, residue from the prior evening or day's activities, work events, relationship issues, night terrors that are so real and vivid that I have difficulty distinguishing them from reality of here and now, and any core needs such as safety, shelter, food, sleep, or employment/financial security that are met, unmet, or undefined may sideline any purposeful goals of the day.

My daily purpose is also determined by my innermost needs to be/feel valued and a general sense of making this life worthwhile and authentic to my true self. When I reflect on how I am currently being able to maintain authenticity in my daily interactions, I often become overwhelmed by a sense of cognitive dissonance and in incongruent wage-earnings activities that have side-tracked me into a life not worth living. That being said; my utmost goal is to keep finding a reason to stay alive and to embrace a life of vibrant energy, joy, and commitment to self.

I often wonder during those early morning musings whether or not it is truly worth getting up and driving to work, or if I should just "cash it in" and give up, surrender to the life that is without meaning and/or purpose and wait for the Creator of all life to throw me a new life challenge. Maybe I need a new challenge in order to create meaning in this life, maybe not. I don't know. Sometimes I think how wonderful it would all be just to lie down under a tree with a blanket wrapped around me and sleep until the cows come home. Man is that a wonderful thought! So inviting, right?

I used to do just that when I was a kid. I would sleep in the woods, even in the winter. I would make a bed out of cedar or pine branches and leaves, cover myself with another layer of the branches and sleep peacefully. Often I would wake up to see either deer or rabbits beside me, watching me sleep. My beagle dogs would also come sleep beside me there, in the woods, under the cedar trees in the bed that was just the right size for a little girl, where a deer had slept peacefully. The air smelled gloriously fresh, no cigarette smoke! And for that brief time, I would know that I was safe, hidden from those who would harm me. My only peace in a chaotic life of a little girl too young to understand, yet wise in the ways of cruelty of those who were supposed to protect her, but violated her daily.

Last Word

I had to capture that smart aleck attitude that pisses me off and makes me laugh. The poem was written several years later after I dug out the quotes from my journal. For Vinny, my Vinny, the wisecracker.
-Dawn Cunningham

Last Word

"***Pick*** up the ***floor***," Mom huffs.

      I told my head, and
      "Iiiii caaaaaan't," whines
      through my lips,
      off my palate.
      I shrug. "The floor
      is too heavy," smirking under
      my now rolled eyes. Mom back-
      draft of guttural sounds
      at my back:

        "PICK UP"

          Then she huffs the big bad wolf,

           "that"

          To bring hardest puff

          "FLOOR!"

           And I whisper, "breathe."

Ethiopian Justice

I had been in Asmara, the capital of Eritrea, processing into my next military assignment. Eritrea was controlled by the Germans and Italians during the late 1930s and through the end of World War II. Afterward, the League of nations (presently the United Nations), placed Eritrea under the control of Emperor Haile Selassie's Ethiopian government and military. Other cities and outlying villages were patrolled by Ethiopian Police or Game Wardens. In the outlying villages, there were local uprisings to gain back the independence of Eritrea. The organization was called ELF, the Eritrean Liberation Front. So much for part of my in-processing.

- John D. Hannigan

Ethiopian Justice

The Ethiopian Judicial System did have a court, judge, and a small prison. Depending on the nature of the crime, the court would assign the punishment. The typical punishment for a minor offense was the loss of a knuckle on the person's left hand for each offense. This showed his countrymen that he was a thief and could not be trusted. The more he stole, the more knuckles were removed. Should he continue to steal, he would lose knuckles up to his ring finger. Eventually, he would lose his left hand, forcing him to die or eat with his dirty right hand. The typical punishment for a major crime, such as adultery, murder, or trying to overthrow the Ethiopian government was death by hanging.

I had been in Asmara about four days into my processing when the American community, if not on military duty, was told by the American Consulate to attend the next morning in Bosch, the local marketplace. The weather was cool, in the 70s, a typical morning on the mountain top. My wife and I left the hotel and walked the half-mile downtown to the market area, not knowing what to expect. We joined the other Americans who were there. Members of the other countries' Embassies were there as well. A large part of the Italian Community had closed their businesses so they could be in attendance. The Bosch was barren; local Eritrean shops and vendor books that were normally open were closed.

As the crowd began assembling, local Eritreans gathered along with the Swedish, Italian, English and American communities as requested by the Ethiopian government to witness what was going to be taking place. Shortly before 9:00 a.m., one could hear different dialects being spoken by the gathering crowd in normal conversation. The local Eritreans were dressed in their white clothing, similar to what Americans would call cheesecloth. The other countries were also dressed in their native attire. The crowd was calming, waiting.

There were four gallows and a podium standing in front of them in the center of the Bosch. The Ethiopian official mounted the podium and the crowd quieted down to a hush. The trial commenced with the Ethiopian official reading from a document, his voice loud and firm as he read the charges in the local Eritrean-Aramaic language. Four Eritrean women were being charged with prostitution and infecting Ethiopian soldiers with venereal disease. There was no defense attorney for the women. The Ethiopian official's verdict was death by hanging.

From a ridge where the local prison was, a drumbeat began as the Ethiopian soldiers marched four female prisoners to the gallows. The women were screaming along the way. The official kept reading from his paper, repeating the charges to the people present in an intimidating manner to remind the local Eritreans what could happen to them if they committed the same crimes against the Ethiopian government.

As each woman approached, screaming, she would be handcuffed, led up the stairs and a noose placed over her head. The crowd was quiet and reserved during the reading and as the women went to the gallows. Finally the Ethiopian official finished reading the charges. The trap doors were opened under each gallows and the women's bodies dropped, they still screaming as their bodies twisted in their death throes before becoming limp. My wife grabbed my arm and let out a scream, and I turned my head away.

The limp bodies hung in the Bosch all day so the entire communities around Asmara could witness Ethiopian government law and justice to the Eritrean citizens. Some of the local citizens, Italians, English, and Swedish left the Bosch to open their businesses or go back to their Embassies. Others stayed and stood in fear of what could happen to them if they did not obey Ethiopian law. There was an uproar from the crowd, not a riot, to show the Ethiopian government their displeasure with the trial.

My wife and I left and returned to our hotel. We discussed the executions of the women. It was certainly something that we had not experienced in our lifetimes. It was our first witnessing to a public hanging, and hopefully the last Ethiopian justice that we had witnessed. It also showed us for the first time that each country has a very different Judicial System from the United States. The United States would arrest and maybe give a short sentence to a female who was a prostitute; but public hanging was definitely not considered. While we were in Eritrea, we were also governed by the Ethiopian Judicial System.

That night we found out from another American couple who had been in the country a few years that if an Eritrean woman engages in sexual activity prior to marriage, she is an outcast for life by her tribe and is not allowed to marry. This must have been the cause for these four women. Prostitution was now allowed in the Eritrean community and is considered under Ethiopian Justice as a crime to be dealt with a prison term and the penalty of death by hanging.

There were several religions in Eritrea; moderate Islamic, Coptic Christians, Jews, Roman Catholics, and Protestant Missionaries trying to convert local inhabitants into their religions. Many of these forbade sexual activity before marriage.

The infected Ethiopian soldiers were never identified, and I do not know if they were ever punished according to Ethiopian law and their religious beliefs. I would assume that they would be covered by the same laws as the women, however, I believe that they were not charged.

One Thing to Choose

We had the assignment "If you could have one thing to keep with you always, what would it be, and why?" It was an interesting and difficult writing prompt for me because, as a military member, I have gone many times without things; so I could not at first decide what it would be. I also could not think of a feeling I would want to keep with me, for that would make me not appreciate some other things.

Finally, something came to me at once, and I began writing.
- ML Wissing

One Thing to Choose

If I could have anything,
Anything at all,
Forever with me,
Never to fall.

Would I choose something tangible,
Something I could touch,
Would I choose a feeling,
One I'd feel so much?

Would it make me smile
When all the world is blue,
Would it make me sing
When everything is out of tune?

In a world so possession-based
In a world that is so greedy,
If I could just have one thing
Would it help me be less needy?

Perhaps I could wish for love
Never to leave my heart
Perhaps maybe duct tape
So I don't fall apart.

But I cannot think of anything
To forever be by my side,
For if something never leaves you
You don't appreciate the ride.

With only happiness and laughter,
You do not feel the pain,
With only sunshine and daisies

You cannot appreciate the rain.

When only peace survives,
There isn't any war
But you won't appreciate it,
Not the way you did before.

If you only keep one thing
Forever by side,
How do you appreciate the time
You had when the shadow died?

I could wish forever
Time in my love's embrace,
But how would I know
If he held my true love's face?

So many things I could choose
So many on the list,
But to choose one thing forever
I could not choose this.

Without the bright colors,
You could not like the dark blues.
Perhaps the one thing I need to keep
Is the free will just to choose.

I was able, through my job as the Director of IPFW's military Student Services, to bring Silouan Green to our campus to speak to our students, staff, and faculty over a year ago. After hearing his story and getting copies of his workbook, *The Ladder UPP™,* I recruited some help from the IPFW faculty and staff who were published authors and instructors to brainstorm the beginnings of the Ladder UPP™ Creative Writing Group. We opened the group to any person from the university or surrounding areas of Northeast Indiana who had experience with PTSD to join the group and share the writing as we worked through the workbook. The membership has changed many times since we began, as group members' attendance has fluctuated and new faces were added.

The work we do each week inspires me to keep on keeping on, doing what I do as an administrator, colleague, a family member, and as an individual. I experience a bundle of PTSD from a variety of source events and illnesses. I am a survivor—of many difficult events, relationships, illnesses, and living circumstances. The Ladder UPP™ helps me to become not only a survivor, but an OVERCOMER!
-J. Vaughan

I Am Sitting as I Am

As it is with many of my poems, evening time and late night brings out me. I had been working on a blog when this poem began to ramble from my fingers.
- Dawn Cunningham

I Am Sitting As I Am

I am random. Randomness is me.

I am the woods and I am the pasture;
 I am the tree and I am the granite;
   I am the stillness and I am the motion;
     I am all and I am none:

        my mind fuses and chips into phrases that fall
like tinted leaves:
        my selfhood attempts to survive with multi-
personalities found
        on my tongue, telling me
        to shut up when one decides to speak.

    I am an ocean roaring inside the
      I-am-the-river flowing outside the
        I-am-who I do not appear to be;
        I am exactly as I appear to be;
          I am as I am as you are as you are not;
           I am every letter in every alphabet without an
escape to speak

Baby Bat
(3-24-16)

-Denise K. Buhr

". . . I laughed so hard I think I sprained my face."
- Brian Doyle's 96-year-old friend

Baby Bat
(3-29-16)

Given what the library looks like in its deconstruction phase (that is, demolition), it's not surprising that bats would find a home there. Last Friday, I was at the reference consulting desk in the Library Services Center, the former 24-hour computer lab, when someone said, "We have a bat on the first floor!" The LSC is a separate, enclosed room with full length windows on the inside wall. Those allow a good, and safe, view of what's happening on the first floor. And on Friday it was a lost baby bat trying to find its way home.

It flew around the hallway outside the windows, toward the temporary wall at the end, past the elevator doors into the main floor, then back again. Around and around, occasionally landing on the floor to rest, sometimes hanging from the brick around the elevators. At one point one of the elevators' doors opened and three construction workers stepped out. And ducked as the bat swooped down at them. After the first moments of being startled, they didn't seem too concerned and went on their way to the main part of the floor, while the bat continued flying in the hallway.

Temporary walls were built to create a sort of safe corridor from the bridge doors on the second floor for students and staff to get to the Honors Center and to the south stairwell. There is another temporary wall at the end of the first floor leading from the stairwell to the LSC. However, as someone pointed out, none of the walls go all the way to the ceiling. What if the bat flew over the top of the wall? And at that point it did. It must be noted that the doors to the stairwell are constantly propped open. Now there was a scramble for the phones.

Call Physical Plant—tell them to send someone over to catch it.

Call Honors—warn them to keep their doors closed.

Call the Library Admin office (in the conference room at the end of the bridge)—apprise them of the situation.

Call the information desk, also at the end of the bridge
—tell them to keep their eyes open and their heads down! "Wait, what do you mean you don't believe us? It's true! I'm telling you!" Moments later a call comes back from the two female student workers at that desk. "Can you bring up sanitizing wipes? It landed on the desk! Right in front of me! And walked all over the place! Is that laughter I hear?" Yes, yes it was. Those of us in the safety of the LSC were in tears!

In the meantime, the three construction workers came back and asked about it. We sent them off to follow its trail of terror. After launching from the service desk, it flew down the bridge and into the student union. (Call my officemates in Walb G25—keep a lookout when you leave!) The next report, from the construction guys – they caught it and released it outside.

Nothing like a little fright and a lot of laughter to end the week. Only two things would have made the whole episode even better. To have actually seen the reactions of the two young women at the information desk, maybe gotten it on video. And if the bridge had been full of students! Oh, the horror, the panic, the brash young heroes who might have tried to save the day or cowered under the tables! But at 4 pm on a Friday there were only a few scattered students left and they probably didn't even notice the baby bat.

Letter to the Editor

   The Fort Wayne Parks & Recreation Department and Indiana Tech School proposed to lease part of Memorial Park from the city to build a sport complex and a ladies' softball field.

   The proposal was to remove dedicated trees as well as to level the hill where the World War I monument stands for men and women from Allen County who served.

   A public hearing was held on May 4th, 2017 which allowed citizens and veterans to state several pros and cons. The discussions resulted in Indiana Tech School withdrawing their proposal and the creation of a workgroup to consider improvements to the memorial.
   - John D. Hannigan

Memorial Park Proposal

5 May, 2017

I relocated to Fort Wayne in 1968 when Magnavox hired me. Fort Wayne was smaller then. There have been many changes in Fort Wayne since 1968. The city has grown and most industry has deteriorated even though the city has grown. My family frequented Memorial Park many time to pay respect to the World War I veterans that Memorial Park commemorates and honors. I played softball in an industrial league for many years in the park. I participated in Veteran Memorial Services in the park.

I will say upfront that I do not agree with the current Fort Wayne Parks and Recreation Department and the Indiana Tech proposal. Memorial Park is Hallowed Grounds and should be maintained in its current configuration. Let us do some historical research of Memorial Park.

A person gave the City of Fort Wayne a tract of her land and dedicated it to the World War I veterans in 1919. The Parks and Recreation Department had the responsibility to maintain this tract of land. A few years later in 1922, the World War I Memorial was erected and 125 trees were planted to honor Fort Wayne Citizens who was put in Harms-Way in Europe and gave the ultimate sacrifice for the United States of America. Thereby, memorializing the park as a more sacred hallow ground than any of the City's many cemeteries that honors the citizens and veterans of the Fort Wayne Community.

It is my understanding that about one hundred of the trees planted to honor the citizens that gave their life in WWI no longer exist. Why those trees were never replanted by the Parks and Recreation Department to honor the fallen is a travesty.

Indiana Tech, you have improved the east side of Fort Wayne with your beautiful campus and surrounding. In 1968, an A&P Grocery store sat where your campus sits now. It was firebomb during the 1960' riots that hurt the growth of downtown Fort Wayne. Although, the Memorial Park is the best location you have chosen to extend your campus and develop a sports complex, it is not the right location for your expansion. Please consider another location for your new venture. A site closer to the campus will only improve the Fort Wayne East Side and add to the beautification of the community.

Fort Wayne citizens and veterans please participate in the Public Hearing on June 1st at Citizens Center at 6:00PM to voice your pros/cons of the Parks and Recreation Department and Indiana Tech's proposal to change the atmosphere of Memorial Park.

    John Hannigan
    Army Veteran 1953 - 1964

You Came in the Mail

This was a strange moment, not knowing what to do. Vincent [my son] was in my hands, smaller than a baby. How would I take this moment?
- Dawn Cunningham

You Came in the Mail

You come back in a black box wrapped in brown paper in a sealed white package. Lifting you is lifting a newborn baby—one hundred forty-six pounds turned into six pounds, less than your actual birth weight. I'm afraid to lift you, thinking you will fall from my fingers and spill to the ground, losing you again. You're compressed like a file stored deep into the system of a computer. The lid of the black box is taped with the same tape used to protect electronic boards when packaged in bubbles. There are no bubbles surrounding you like the first time you discovered how soap makes bubbles in the bathtub. Nor are there the bubbles from the bubble wrap you ran across, sounding like a tiny automatic pistol. As I move the compressed you, I expect sound to escape, like a moo box or a jack in the box with the head popping out. This package delivered to me holds every memory we created, and I cannot reach in to pull any of those memories out of you.

Please Hear Me

Growing up, I didn't always hear the loving words I needed to. I was called the "Devil's Child" so often that I began to believe it. Verbal, physical, and sexual abuses only made my self-appreciation and self-worth hit rock bottom, leaving me feeling as if I was worth little more than trash.

Now I realize that as long as I love myself, I am loved by the most important person in my own life. If I am proud of my own accomplishments, I am a success. I am loved and appreciated.

It is a truly wonderful feeling.
-ML Wissing

Please Hear Me

It's the little things that you don't realize are there; moments that last only tenths of a second, breaths between heartbeats, that you don't even think about, don't even acknowledge as even existing, that end up being the most moving, the most remembered in hindsight.

It is in these moments that history of a person, of the people around them, of the world around them, are touched, and in that touch, the world is changed forever for them. They are the times that, now that you look back, hold a profound impact upon your mind, sticking out like a flower in the snow, so obvious now that you see it, yet while you were there, it wasn't to be seen.

Looking back, there were hundreds of those moments.

Moments that I should have seen, but in my walking my own path, I failed to look around and see the flowers in the snow around me.

They haunt my memory now, not as ghosts, but as reminders, to gather and hold dear to my heart, and to pass these moments on, and make sure they are received, that they are seen, and that hopefully are appreciated.

Moments when words like "I'm so proud of you," "I am here for you," and "I love you," are needed in a person's life, not as mere words, but as those moments that will help impact their mind so profoundly, that they look back on those moments, and remember and smile.

With each impact upon a human heart, each gentle touch upon their soul, you not only touch them, but the people around them, and the world around them. You not only impact one person.... you impact the world.

Make every moment count, make every moment memorable.

And never forget...

I am proud of you, I am here for you....

And I love you.

Afterword

*We hope you have gained as much from reading our
book as we have in writing it.*

The Ladder UPP™

You are not alone!

Life can break anyone. We all take hits. The impact can be as varied as our human experience and I have found that unresolved brokenness leads to a muddling life at best, severe mental health issues at worst.

It can happen in many ways: how we are raised, life trauma, loss of a loved one, war, assault, addiction, bullying, you name it. To live again, we must learn how to live free. That is what The Ladder UPP™ does, it is the first step to a new life where we are free to truly live. Once we begin stepping forward our paths will diverge based on our own particular passions and purpose, but to get moving, we need to figure out how to overcome our past and learn to look forward in a smart, healthy way.

Where are you going?

Whether you just aren't happy with life, or you are suffering from conditions like depression or PTSD, you must REVEAL your true self by looking at your past, present and future honestly and with transparency. Then you must REBUILD your life by ordering your life clearly and simply, setting goals, and looking forward with passion and purpose. Finally, you must START THE JOURNEY by taking that first step with a clear plan and others who will hold you accountable. Those are the steps The Ladder UPP™ leads one through – REVEAL, REBUILD, START THE JOURNEY – and those are the steps that build the foundation of a life that is free.

The Ladder UPP™ has been used by veterans, survivors of those lost serving our country, retired folks and young people looking for purpose, sexual assault victims, police officers, counselors, children, prisoners, you name it. The Ladder UPP™ is for anyone who wants to learn to live with deep passion and purpose, or as I like to say, those who want to live free.

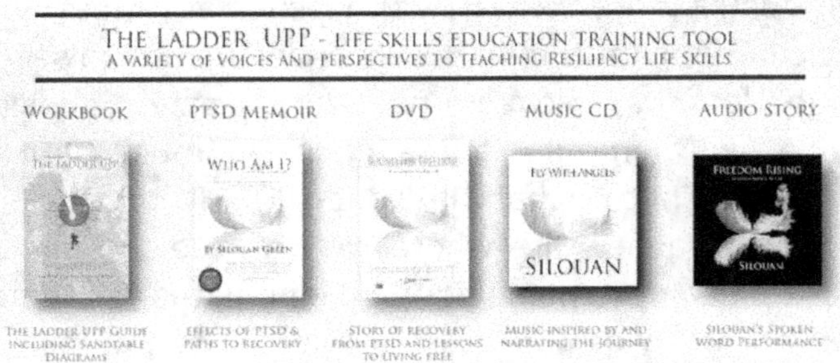

The Ladder Upp™
http://www.silouan.com/the-ladder-upp